MING'S
MASTER
RECIPES

Published by Ming East-West, LLC

Printed in the United States of America

Library of Congress Cataloging-in-Publication Data is available upon request

ISBN 0-9761004-0-1

10 9 8 7 6 5 4 3 2 1

First Edition

To Mom & Pops:
Thank you for putting me on this planet
and for showing me that food is life.

To Polly:
Thank you for putting David and Henry
on this planet and for showing me
that there is _more_ to life than food,
so much more.

Simply Ming Crew

ACKNOWLEDGMENTS

To fabulous co-executive producers Laurie Donnelly and Julia Harrison, the boat-dwelling director Jeff Kaye, editor-extraordinaire Dave Allen, Super Woman Chef Joanne O'Connell, the ever-resourceful Chris Cavalieri, point person Deb Hurley, ultra-reliable Hilary Finkel, Scott Wolfeil—who lights better than anyone in the biz, Louise Daniels Miller who keeps my mug camera-worthy, master publicist Dustin Smith and Aaron Caramanis—the prop stylist of stylists, in addition to the whole Simply Ming crew, a HUGE thank you. Without this team, there would be no book and no show!

To the two ladies that keep Ming East-West running: Susan Canning, who keeps my life organized, and Sarah Hearn, for putting this beautiful book together.

To all the guest chefs: Colin Cowie, Gale Gand, Hiroko Shimbo, Jacques Pepin, Jasper White, Joanne Chang, Ken Oringer, Lidia Bastianich, Martin Yan, Melissa Kelly, Michael Lomonaco, Michael Schlow, Susur Lee, Todd English, and especially my parents, Mom & Pops—I thank you for your tasty recipes and friendships.

Last but certainly not least, the entire Blue Ginger team including Jon Taylor, Isaac Bancaco, Tom Woods, pastry chef extraordinaire Marina Brancely, Michele Fadden, Paula Pearson, and Sarah Livesey—a special Merci to Tom Finigan and Ayoub El Fougani for their wine expertise.

Simply Ming Crew: Amelia Battaglio, Bill Fairweather, Brant Fagan, Brendan Keefe, Chris Bresnahan, Chris Merlo, Denise Swidey, Elizabeth Tyson, Frank Coakley, Gilles Morin, Han Quach, Jill Santopietro, Joel Coblenz, Jonathan Kobs, Kate Hathaway, Kathy Gleason, Kelsey Clark, Laryn Ivy, Larry Lecain, Marianne Tacito, MaryAnn Janke, Michael Gaines (for the awesome food photography), Michael Mulvey, Michael Tivey, Nick Cocuzzo, Patrick Kelly, Rob Matthews, Sacha Shawky, Stephen Hussar, Thomas Joseph, Todd Seyfarth, Tommy Hamilton.

MASTER RECIPE
Garlic-Ginger-Scallion Stir Fry Sauce
P.E.I. Mussels and Chinese Sausage, page 24

TABLE OF CONTENTS

RECIPE INDEX

INTRODUCTION

I ALWAYS SAY A PICTURE IS WORTH A THOUSAND WORDS, especially in cookbooks, so I am incredibly pleased with this companion book to SIMPLY MING, season 2. The pictures throughout this book were actually shot "on set". As soon as the cameras stopped rolling, we photographed the dishes "live" and only then were we allowed to dig in! Like *Simply Ming*, I continue with the Master Recipe system, presenting 20 new ones, each with 2 to 3 dishes. The guest chefs that joined me on the show continually wowed me with their creativity, adding their own touches and creating amazing dishes with my Masters and I've included those recipes as well.

The response I received from the first book and season of the show has been tremendous. People have really responded to this system which makes East-West cooking an easy possibility any night of the week—my goal! When my first book *Blue Ginger* came out, East-West cuisine was still on the periphery, considered by many to be trendy and faddish—too exotic for mainstream. In the past six years, there has been a definite evolution in Americans' eating and cooking habits: people want tasty food, they like using different spices and produce, and Asian ingredients are increasingly easy to buy—no special trips to Chinatown required! This is food that is not as much about ethnicity as it is about taste, texture, and freshness. The Cranberry-Teriyaki Glaze, Garlic-Ginger-Scallion Stir Fry Sauce, and Jasmine Caramel Sauce are just a few of the Masters that will pack flavor, color, and aromas into your next meal, easily transforming chicken, sweet potatoes, and even vanilla ice cream into unique and delectable culinary pleasures.

Be sure to read the Tips when you begin using this book—they include helpful information on how to approach the Master Recipe system. I hope this new set of Masters will have more people enjoying cooking and eating in their homes with family and friends. Of course, I will consider this book a true success if you take the Masters and create your own dishes, adding your personality and culture to the dishes, because at the end of the day, these recipes are simply a guide, there to serve as inspiration. Remember, you are doing the cooking, so cook what you like. It is your kitchen after all!

Peace & Good Eating.
Ming Tsai

TIPS FOR USING THIS BOOK

◆ The best way to approach this cookbook and master recipe system is to begin by looking through the list of dishes and noting ones that appeal to you. Then look at the master recipe, note the ingredients needed and figure out a convenient time to make a batch. I find that the weekends are the perfect time—then you are set for the week ahead. With that flavor base made and stored, plan your shopping list for multiple meals, eliminating extra trips to the market. And of course, remember how long you may safely store the master recipe.

◆ For the majority of dishes, one batch of the master will be enough to make all of the recipes it's designed for. If you are a household of two or one, feel free to halve any of the masters—they are all designed to be easily doubled or halved, as needed.

◆ I've always been a huge fan of matching wines with food. With each master, I've included two beverage recommendations that show off their versatility and paired each dish accordingly. Keep in mind that this is simply a guide and that at the end of the day you should drink whatever you'd like! There are wonderful teas, fresh juices, and sparkling waters that are just as great with these dishes.

◆ Plastic quart and pint containers that deli salads come in make perfect storage containers for the majority of master recipes. Screw-top glass jars—such as large empty mayonnaise jars or mason jars are also great. Just be sure that they are clean and that you label the date on them.

◆ Always use a spoon or chopsticks to taste—placing a finger in the master ingredients can introduce unwanted bacteria.

MASTER RECIPE

Many are huge fans of teriyaki
sauce, loving the salty-sweet flavor
it gives to meat and chicken. I've added
fresh citrus and tangy cranberries (an ode
to New England) to my version, producing
a smooth glaze with body that adds
tons of flavor to your dishes—just
brush it on and cook!

CRANBERRY-TERIYAKI GLAZE

Makes 3 cups

1 large red onion, sliced

1 tablespoon minced ginger

1 cup dried cranberries, such as Craisins

Zest and juice of 1 orange

1 cup naturally brewed soy sauce

2 cups cranberry juice

½ cup sugar

¼ cup grapeseed or canola oil for cooking

Kosher salt and freshly ground black pepper, to taste

In a sauce pan coated lightly with oil over high heat, sauté the onions, ginger and dried cranberries until soft, about 5 minutes. Add the orange zest and juice, naturally brewed soy sauce, cranberry juice, and sugar and bring to a simmer. Reduce by 50 percent over low heat, about 10 to 15 minutes. Check for flavor. Immediately, transfer to a blender and blend until almost smooth (with small bits is preferable), drizzling in the oil. Do not blend until super smooth. Check for flavor and adjust seasonings. Let come to room temperature, then transfer to a glass jar, seal and store in fridge for up to two weeks.

RECOMMENDED BEVERAGES

Newton Unfiltered Merlot

Where: Sonoma, California
Grape: Merlot
Style: This merlot is less fruity and jammy than some of the newer ones, leaning more towards being richer and darker while exhibiting black fruit flavors. It is wonderful with fruit-based sauces and glazes, making it an ideal match for these dishes using the Cranberry-Teriyaki Glaze.

Concha y Toro Carmenere

Where: Maipo, Chile
Grape: Carmenere
Style: This type of wine has been called a merlot for generations in Chile where it is known as the "6th Bordeaux Grape". It is a medium-bodied red that still retains a certain meatiness that bonds well with dishes like lamb. Chilean wines are gaining popularity as they are great wines that are still very affordable.

Seven years ago I was on a cooking show competing against good friend and phenomenal chef Susur Lee. I was given raisins, chicken, and soy sauce and created a raisin teriyaki sauce: the raisins plumped up and when puréed, the sauce became wonderfully thick and absolutely awesome on chicken. I've substituted tart Craisins for raisins with equally tasty results. The garlicky bok choy is a wonderful foil for the sweet cranberry teriyaki—and very healthy too!

CRANBERRY-TERIYAKI CHICKEN ON GARLIC BOK CHOY

Serves 4

4 boneless chicken breasts, skin on
1 cup Cranberry-Teriyaki Glaze, save 2 tablespoons for garnish
3 cloves garlic, thinly sliced
5 large heads baby bok choy, cored, split in half and cut into ¼-inch slices (may substitute napa cabbage)
1 teaspoon sesame oil (optional)
Grapeseed or canola oil for cooking
Kosher salt and freshly ground black pepper, to taste

Prepare a hot grill or broiler. On a large plate, brush the breasts with the glaze on both sides. Season the breasts and grill them on both sides until cooked through, about 5 minutes a side, brushing frequently with the glaze. Let chicken rest for 3 to 5 minutes before slicing on the bias. Meanwhile, in a wok or sauté pan coated lightly with oil over high heat, add the garlic then bok choy. Move around quickly, season with kosher salt and freshly ground black pepper and check for seasoning. Keep the bok choy al dente and drizzle with sesame oil, about 3 minutes total.
On 4 plates, place a small mound of the bok choy and top with the sliced chicken. Zig-zag remaining glaze over the plates.

Serve with: *Newton Unfiltered Merlot*

CRANBERRY-TERIYAKI LAMB RACK WITH COUSCOUS SALAD

Gamey meats such as the succulent lamb rack are constantly paired with fresh and dried fruits with absolutely delicious results. Glazing the lamb with the Cranberry-Teriyaki keeps the meat wonderfully moist and adds another dimension of flavor—glazing is a technique we use often at Blue Ginger. The couscous salad is a nod to the traditional Moroccan couscous and dried fruit duo and a great accompaniment to the lamb.

Serves 4

2 naturally fed lamb racks, fat cap removed
1 cup Cranberry-Teriyaki Glaze
2 cups couscous, cooked
Juice and zest of 1 lemon
1 tablespoon of Dijon mustard
¼ cup extra virgin olive oil
3 scallion stalks sliced, white and green parts separated
¼ cup dried cranberries, such as Craisins, chopped
1 red or green jalapeño, stemmed and minced with the seeds
Kosher salt and freshly ground black pepper, to taste
Grapeseed or canola oil for cooking

Marinate the racks in the glaze overnight. Preheat an oven to 450°F and place a heavy bottom pan over medium heat. Season the racks with kosher salt and freshly ground black pepper. Coat pan lightly with oil and sear all sides of the rack, about 8 minutes, and transfer to the oven. Roast for 5 to 8 additional minutes for medium rare to medium. Meanwhile, in a large bowl, whisk together juice, zest and Dijon. Add oil and season with kosher salt and freshly ground black pepper to taste. Mix in scallion whites, cranberries, and jalapeños, then couscous, and toss to combine. Let lamb rest 5 to 8 minutes before slicing. Place a small mound of couscous salad on plates, top with lamb chops, and garnish with scallion greens. Serve with extra Cranberry-Teriyaki Glaze.

Serve with: *Concho y Toro Carmenere*

Cranberry-Teriyaki Lamb Rack with Couscous Salad   7

CRANBERRY-TERIYAKI SWEET POTATO SATAYS

In China, they sell glazed crab apples on the street. In this recipe, however, sugary sweet potatoes are glazed with the sweet-tart-savory Cranberry-Teriyaki and sprinkled with chives and sesame seeds. The flavor combination will blow you away and I think you'll agree that this is the best way to prepare sweet potatoes—simply unbelievable!

Serves 4, as an appetizer

2 large sweet potatoes or yams, baked with skin on, until al dente, about 45 minutes at 350°F
1 cup Cranberry-Teriyaki Glaze
¼ cup chopped chives
2 tablespoons sesame seeds
Satay skewers soaked in water

Prepare a hot and cleaned grill. Peel the potatoes whole and make ½-inch long slices. Skewer the potato slices and dip in the glaze. Sprinkle with chives and sesame seeds and grill on both sides until well colored, about 4 minutes a side. Serve satays stuck in a potato that has been sliced in half and use like a pin cushion.

Serve with: *Concho y Toro Carmenere*

Review of Show with Crew

LIDIA BASTIANICH'S OVEN-BRAISED PORK CHOPS WITH RED ONIONS, PEARS AND CRANBERRY-TERIYAKI SAUCE (COSTOLETTE DI MAIALE BRASATE AL FORNO CON PERE)

Lidia is a veteran of public television and a matriarch of Italian-American cuisine. Her dish is a gorgeous comforting meal that captures all the wonderful tastes of autumn: red onions, cranberries, pears, and prime center cut pork chops. The sugar in the Cranberry-Teriyaki Glaze helps to caramelize the pork, onions, and pears as they braise, producing a wonderful depth of flavor. Served with mashed butternut squash, this is a hearty meal with refined flavors and vibrant colors.

Serves 4

2 cups Cranberry-Teriyaki Glaze, reduced to syrupy consistency
3 tablespoons extra virgin olive oil
6 garlic cloves, peeled
4 center cut pork rib chops, each about 12 ounces and 1¼-inches thick
1 large red onion (about 12 ounces), cut into 8 wedges
Salt and freshly ground pepper
2 ripe but firm Bosc pears, peeled, cored and cut into 8 wedges
2 cups mashed butternut squash

Preheat oven to 425° F. Heat the oil in a large, heavy skillet with a flameproof handle over medium-high heat. Whack the garlic cloves with the flat side of a knife and scatter them over the oil. Cook, shaking the skillet, until brown, about 2 minutes. Lay the pork chops in the skillet and cook until the underside is browned, about 6 minutes. Remove and reserve the garlic cloves if they become more than deep golden brown before the chops are fully browned. Turn over the chops, tuck the onion wedges into the pan and continue cooking until the second side of the chops is browned, about 6 minutes. Season with salt and pepper. About halfway through browning the second side, tuck the pear wedges in between the chops.

Return the garlic cloves to the skillet if you have removed them and add Cranberry-Teriyaki Glaze. Place the skillet in the oven and roast until the onions and pears are tender and the juices from the pork are a rich, syrupy dark brown, about 30 minutes. Once or twice during roasting, turn the chops and redistribute the onions and pears. Handle the skillet carefully—it will be extremely hot. Remove the skillet from the oven. Check the seasoning of the onion-pear mixture, adding salt and pepper if necessary. Place a mound of mashed butternut squash in center of each warmed serving plate and spoon the pears, onions and pan juices over squash. Top with a pork chop and drizzle plate with more sauce if desired.

Serve with: *Newton Unfiltered Merlot*

MASTER RECIPE

*I have always loved tea smoking—
a classic Chinese cooking technique—for the
wonderful smoky flavor it imparts on food. Here
I've combined a fruity blackberry tea with curry powder. Fruit and curry is always a great combination,
especially in the Indian tradition—think of all those
wonderful chutneys! While I was in South Africa, I
toured the famous spice markets of Durban, which are
filled with aromatic and colorful Indian spices—South
Africa has an enormous Indian influence. While many
home cooks steer clear of Indian cuisine, this Curry Tea
Rub gives you the wonderful flavor of India with
minimum fuss or expense. Just rub the curry spice
blend on chicken, fish, meat or veggies and then
cook—in no time you have a unique and tasty
dish and it doesn't get much easier than that!*

CURRY TEA RUB

Makes 3 cups

> 1¼ cups Madras curry or any local curry powder
>
> ½ cup turbinado sugar
>
> ½ cup blackberry tea or any local fruity tea
>
> 2 tablespoons ground ginger
>
> ½ cup sea salt
>
> ¼ cup chives
>
> ¼ cup lime zest

In a small bowl, mix all the ingredients together. Store in a covered glass jar in a dry, dark place for up to 1 month.

RECOMMENDED BEVERAGES

Rust En Vrede Malbec

Where: Stellenbosch, South Africa
Grape: Malbec
Style: This wine features an incredibly dark red color with intense blackberry and peppered fennel notes, fine ripe tannins, and a long warm finish. This is ideal with rich red meats as well as ostrich and venison.

Mulderbosch Sauvignon Blanc

Where: Stellenbosch, South Africa
Grape: Sauvignon Blanc
Style: Possessing a lively golden-green color, this wine is packed with gooseberry, papaya, and pineapple. Its powerful and concentrated taste has become a trademark of Mulderbosch. This is one of my all-time favorite wines to pair with butterfish.

I am a huge fan of Alaskan butterfish—it's the basis for one of my signature dishes at Blue Ginger. Here it is prepared with a coating of Curry Tea Rub—the curry and sweet tea give a wonderful exotic flavor to this mild fish and dried mangoes—a popular item in Indian kitchens—complement the fruity tea and the heat of the curry.

CURRY TEA RUBBED BUTTERFISH WITH DRIED MANGO COUSCOUS

Serves 4

3 cups couscous
¼ cup diced dried mango
½ cup scallions sliced, white and green parts separated
2 tablespoons extra virgin olive oil
3¼ cups boiling water
4 pieces butterfish, 6 to 8 ounces each
½ cup Curry Tea Rub
Grapeseed or canola oil for cooking
Kosher salt and freshly ground black pepper, to taste

In a large bowl, mix together the couscous, mango, scallion whites and extra virgin olive oil. Season with kosher salt and freshly ground black pepper to taste. Add the boiling water, stir and cover immediately with plastic wrap. Let stand 25 to 30 minutes, until couscous is tender. Fluff with the back of a fork and check again for flavor. Meanwhile, pour the Curry Tea Rub onto a plate and press both sides of each piece of fish into the rub. In a sauté pan coated lightly with oil over high heat, sear the fish until the rub is browned and crispy. Turn over fish and continue to sear until cooked through, about 5 minutes a side. Place a small mound of the fluffy couscous on a plate, top with fish and garnish with scallion greens.

Serve with: *Mulderbosch Sauvignon Blanc*

I created this dish while in South Africa with chef Rachel Buchner at Sweni Lodge at Singita—a phenomenal hotel—influenced by the traditional brai or barbecues of the region. Ostrich is quite popular there, but duck is a great substitute. Both are wonderfully gamey and delicious with the smoky sweet Curry Tea Rub. Grilled sweet potatoes and a sweet-tart tropical fruit salsa complete this dish.

BBQ CURRY TEA RUBBED OSTRICH WITH GRILLED SWEET POTATO AND TROPICAL FRUIT SALSA

Serves 4

4 8-ounce ostrich steaks (may substitute duck)
1 cup Curry Tea Rub
½ cup guava, diced
½ cup grapefruit, segmented and cut into slivers
½ cup tamarillo fruit, peeled, seeded and chopped
1 tablespoon cilantro
Juice of 1 lime
2 teaspoons canola oil
3 large sweet potatoes, pierced and wrapped in foil
Grapeseed or canola oil for cooking
Kosher salt and freshly ground black pepper, to taste

Coat the ostrich steaks with the Curry Tea Rub and let rest for 1 hour before grilling or roasting. In a medium bowl, combine guava, grapefruit, tamarillo, cilantro, and lime juice and set aside. Cook the ostrich until medium rare (12 to 15 minutes) and let rest before slicing. Meanwhile, place the sweet potatoes on the grill until al dente, about 30 to 40 minutes. Remove from grill and slice into ¼-inch discs. Brush lightly with oil, season with salt and pepper, and place back on the grill for approximately 3 minutes per side. To serve, place grilled sweet potatoes on plate and top with fanned slices of ostrich. Top with a generous dollop of the salsa.

Serve with: *Rust En Vrede Malbec*

Patty Cahill, Richard Story, John Heller, Margaret Williams, Geoffrey Zakarian, and Colin Cowie

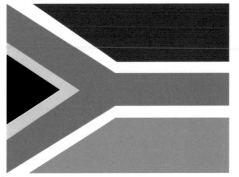

Ming's new South African friends

COLIN COWIE'S SPICED COD WITH TOMATO SAUCE

Serves 2

1 pound cod (2 pieces)
½ cup Curry Tea Rub
3 tablespoons olive oil
1 large shallot, finely chopped
4 plum tomatoes, peeled, seeded and chopped (canned is fine)
1 tablespoon chopped fresh cilantro
¼ cup dry white wine
½ cup low salt chicken or fish stock
Kosher salt and freshly ground black pepper, to taste

Cod and tomatoes are a popular pairing in Mediterranean cuisine—especially in the many delicious seafood stews that abound, such as bouillabaisse and cioppino. Serving the cod in a tasty tomato sauce made with wine, fresh cilantro, shallot, and a pinch of the Curry Tea Rub, keeps the cod moist while the initial searing produces a crispy crust and deep flavor. Some crusty bread and a chilled glass of white wine rounds out this perfect warm-weather meal.

In a medium saucepan, heat 2 tablespoons olive oil over medium-high heat. Add the shallot and 1 teaspoon of the Curry Tea Rub, salt, and pepper and sauté until the shallot is softened and beginning to brown, about 3 minutes. Add the tomatoes and 2 teaspoons of cilantro and continue to cook until the tomatoes begin to give off some of their juice, about 3 to 5 minutes. Add the wine and cook, uncovered, over medium high heat until reduced by half, about 7 minutes. Add the stock, reduce the heat to low and let simmer while you prepare the fish.

Dust cod generously with Curry Tea Rub and let stand for up to 3 hours. Heat the remaining one tablespoon of olive oil in a non-stick frying pan over medium-high heat. Add the fish and cook until well browned, about 3 minutes. Turn fish over and pour the tomato broth around the fish. Let simmer gently until the fish is cooked, about 5 minutes. To serve, transfer the fish to a soup bowl or rimmed plate and ladle broth on top. Sprinkle with remaining cilantro and serve.

Serve with: *Mulderbosch Sauvignon Blanc*

Colin Cowie's Spiced Cod with Tomato Sauce 19

This easy stir fry sauce features three main flavors in Chinese cooking: ginger, garlic, and scallion. Adding this sauce to chicken, seafood, beef, or veggies creates a quick, healthy dinner that is way better than any Chinese takeout.

GARLIC-GINGER-SCALLION STIR FRY SAUCE

Makes 4 cups

½ cup minced garlic

½ cup minced ginger

1 cup scallion, chopped ¼-inch thick

1 cup shaoxing wine

½ cup soy sauce

4 cups chicken stock

2 tablespoons sesame oil

Grapeseed or canola oil to cook

Kosher salt and freshly ground black pepper, to taste

In a wok or sauté pan coated lightly with grapeseed or canola oil over medium-high heat, sauté the garlic, ginger and scallions until soft, about 2 minutes. Deglaze with shaoxing and reduce by 50 percent. Add soy sauce and chicken stock and reduce by 25 percent. Add sesame oil and when cooled, store in a covered glass jar up to two weeks in the fridge.

RECOMMENDED BEVERAGES

William Fevre Chablis

Where: Chablis, France
Grape: Chardonnay
Style: This is an exceptionally crisp wine from the revered Chablis in the northern Burgundy region of France. It is rich with green apple flavors and stony elements and is especially good and affordable at the "premier cru" level.

Bonny Doon "Le Cigare Volent"

Where: Santa Cruz, California
Grape: blend of Syrah, Grenache, and Mourvedre
Style: Though a blend, this wine features predominantly the syrah grape which translates into a mellow fruit with dark undertones of smoke, anise, and leather. The higher acids make it ideal for richer Asian dishes, while the dark flavors work well with ginger, garlic, and scallion.

It is hard to learn how to cook Chinese food without encountering bok choy, a vegetable that has been cultivated in China since ancient times. Although it's considered a member of the cabbage family, it looks nothing like the cabbage we are used to seeing. Its white stalks and dark green leaves are incredibly healthy and its light, sweet flavor and crisp texture make it a delicious addition to many different dishes. A quick sauté in the Garlic-Ginger-Scallion Stir Fry Sauce transforms this vegetable into an awesome and aromatic side dish in minutes.

BOK CHOY 101

Serves 4

8 large heads bok choy, split, cored, soaked in water to clean and spun dried
½ cup Garlic-Ginger-Scallion Stir Fry Sauce
1 tablespoon butter (optional, but recommended)
Grapeseed oil to cook
Kosher salt and freshly ground black pepper, to taste

In a wok or sauté pan coated lightly with oil over high heat, add the bok choy and stir fry for 1 minute. Add the Garlic-Ginger-Scallion Stir Fry Sauce and reduce by 50 percent. Check for seasoning, add butter and serve.

Serve with: *William Fevre Chablis*

Ming Cooking

Surf and turf comes in many incarnations—here is one more to add to your repertoire. With the traditional Portuguese dish Alentejana *that features clams and pork sausage in mind, I created this one which combines fresh-from-the-ocean Prince Edward Island mussels with sweet Chinese sausage in a quick stir fry.*

P.E.I. MUSSELS AND CHINESE SAUSAGE

Serves 4

2 pounds of P.E.I. mussels, cleaned and debearded
2 each Lapchong or Maple sweet breakfast sausage, cut into ¼-inch bias slices
1 large jicama, peeled, sliced, julienned
½ cup Garlic-Ginger-Scallion Stir Fry Sauce
Grapeseed or canola oil to cook
Kosher salt and freshly ground black pepper, to taste
Serve with crusty bread

In a wok or sauté pan, coated lightly with oil over high heat, add the mussels and sauté until slightly opened, about 5 minutes. Add sausage and jicama, sauté for 1 minute, then add the Garlic-Ginger-Scallion Stir Fry Sauce and reduce by 50 percent. Check for flavor. Serve in a large bowl with crusty bread.

Serve with: *William Fevre Chablis*

Stir frys are an excellent solution to the predicament of what to serve during a busy week. They are loaded with flavor, healthy, and adaptable to whatever you have on hand in the kitchen. This one uses chicken and maitake mushrooms, reputed to be the healthiest mushroom in the world. Here we call them "Hen of the Woods" mushrooms. If you can't track any down, oyster mushrooms are a good substitution.

CHICKEN AND MAITAKE MUSHROOM STIR FRY

Serves 4

1 pound skinless, boneless chicken breasts, julienned
1 large head maitake mushroom, stem cleaned and julienned, florets broken off, (may substitute with 1 pound oyster mushrooms)
½ cup Garlic-Ginger-Scallion Stir Fry Sauce
Grapeseed oil to cook
Kosher salt and freshly ground black pepper, to taste
Serve with steamed long grain rice.

In a wok or sauté pan, coated lightly with oil over medium-high heat, stir fry the chicken, moving around quickly, for about 3 minutes over high heat. Add the mushrooms, stir fry 1 minute then add the Garlic-Ginger-Scallion Stir Fry Sauce and reduce by 50 percent. Serve over a mound of rice.

Serve with: *Bonny Doon "Le Cigare Volent"*

MICHAEL LOMONACO'S PECAN-CRUSTED CHICKEN BREAST WITH GARLIC-GINGER-SCALLION VEGETABLE STIR FRY

Michael Lomonaco is one of the best chefs in New York City as well as a great friend, so I was psyched that he could come back and cook with me on the set of Simply Ming. Coating the chicken with pecans gives a wonderful sweet nutty flavor and fun texture. Served with fresh spinach that has been briefly sautéed and tossed with the master Garlic-Ginger-Scallion Stir Fry Sauce adds tons of flavor to this dish.

Serves 4 to 6

2 pounds boneless, skinless chicken breasts
1 cup all-purpose flour
2 eggs
2 tablespoons vegetable oil
2 cups bread crumbs
1 cup pecans, finely chopped
Grapeseed or vegetable oil for frying
1 red pepper, julienned
3 large carrots, sliced into thin "coins"
2 cups cleaned baby spinach leaves
½ cup Garlic-Ginger-Scallion Stir Fry Sauce
Kosher salt and freshly ground black pepper, to taste

Lay each chicken breast, individually, between two pieces of plastic wrap. Using a meat tenderizer or other flat object, pound the chicken breasts to a flat and uniform ½-inch thickness. Set aside and keep cold. Prepare the pecan breading for the chicken. Three separate containers will be needed (preferably flat and wide baking dishes or gratin dishes): one for the flour, one for wet ingredients and one for the breading ingredients.

Place the flour in the first dish. Whisk the eggs together with 2 tablespoons oil and pour into the second dish. Combine the bread crumbs, pecans, salt and pepper in the third dish. Dip the chicken, one at a time, into first the flour, next the egg mixture and finally the pecan breading mix. Try to keep one hand dry and use tongs to transfer the chicken from one dish to another. When all of the chicken has been coated, place on a dish and refrigerate until ready to cook. This may be done in advance.

To cook the chicken, add enough cooking oil to a large skillet to coat the bottom of the pan with ⅛-inch of oil. Heat over medium heat until hot but not smoking. Add the chicken to the oil, and cook the pecan-coated breasts in batches. Avoid over-crowding the pan, and cook each batch until golden brown, about 6 minutes on the first side. Turn the chicken over and cook the second side for an additional 6 minutes until the center is cooked and the juices run clear. Transfer to a platter and keep warm. In a wok, heat 2 tablespoons of oil, add the red pepper and carrots and stir fry until al dente. Add the spinach leaves to the hot wok, allowing to wilt over medium heat for 1 minute. Add the Garlic-Ginger-Scallion Stir Fry Sauce to the vegetables and toss to coat well. Remove and keep warm.

Serve each chicken breast on a bed of Garlic-Ginger-Scallion Vegetable Stir Fry.

Serve with: *Bonny Doon "Le Cigare Volent"*

Michael Lomonaco's Pecan-Crusted Chicken Breast with Garlic-Ginger-Scallion Vegetable Stir Fry   29

MASTER RECIPE

*Hot Water Dough is one
of the building blocks of Chinese
cuisine and with it you can make perfect
pot stickers, all kinds of dumplings, both East
and West-style, and even fried dough. I
learned how to make this dough and all
these different dumplings from the
dumpling queen herself, my mom.*

HOT WATER DOUGH

Makes 2 pounds

2 cups water
4 cups all-purpose flour
½ teaspoon salt

To make the dough, bring water to a boil. In a large stainless steel bowl, combine the flour and salt. Slowly add the boiling water in ¼-cup increments, mixing with chopsticks until a ball is formed and the dough is no longer too hot to handle. All the water may not be needed. Knead the dough on a floured work surface until it becomes smooth and elastic, 15 to 20 minutes. Form the dough into a ball, return it to the bowl, and cover it with a damp cloth. Allow the dough to rest for 1 hour.

Note: While the dough must be made and used immediately, the dumplings may be assembled, seared and frozen for up to 1 month. Make dumplings according to recipe, sear and remove from pan. Drain on a paper towel. When cool, wrap in plastic, then foil, and place in a sealable bag. When ready to serve, remove from freezer, place in pan, browned side down, in oil for one minute. Add the water and steam for 6 to 8 minutes per recipe.

RECOMMENDED BEVERAGES

Saison Dupont Vieille Provision

Where : Hainaut Province, Belgium
Style: This Belgian farmhouse ale is a world class example of the Belgian Saisons style. It has a big, fruity bouquet and a dense head. The taste starts out fruity but ends clean and dry with a light, refreshing body.

Heidler Grüner Veltleiner

Where: Kamptal, Austria
Grape: Grüner Veltleiner
Style: This steep rocky vineyard yields some of the most elegant and sophisticated white wines in the world. The stone gray slate soil gives the wine a delicate acidity that perfectly balances the pure peachy fruit.

Pot stickers are one of the most popular appetizers at Chinese restaurants—the combination of soy, scallion, ginger and pork in a hot water dough wrapper is super tasty. Here is a recipe that is just as good if not better than your favorite restaurant, meaning you can have awesome pot stickers whenever you want.

DIM SUM DIPPER

Makes about 1 cup

2 tablespoons sambal
½ cup rice wine vinegar
½ cup soy sauce
1 teaspoon sesame oil

In a small bowl combine the sambal, vinegar, soy sauce, and sesame oil. Mix and use or store in fridge.

PORK AND SHRIMP POT STICKERS

Makes 16 to 18 pot stickers

1 pound naturally fed ground pork
1 pound small shrimp, completely peeled, cut into ¼-inch dice
¾ cup chopped scallions
1 tablespoon minced ginger
2 tablespoons soy sauce
2 teaspoons sesame oil
½ pound Hot Water Dough
Canola or grapeseed oil for cooking
Serve with Dim Sum Dipper (recipe follows)

In a bowl placed within a larger bowl of ice, mix together the pork, shrimp and scallions. Add the ginger, soy sauce and sesame oil. Do not overmix. Take a small sample and pan sear or microwave to taste for seasoning.

To form the wrappers, add flour to the work surface. Divide the dough in half. Shape one portion into a log and roll it back and forth under your palms to make a thin sausage shape measuring about 1-inch in diameter. Cut into ½-inch pieces. One by one, stand each piece on end, flatten the piece with your palm, and roll out to form a circular wrapper about 3-inches in diameter and ¹⁄₁₆-inch thick. Be sure to make the edges a little thinner than the center so that when the edges are folded over themselves to enclose the filling, they'll still be the same thickness as the rest of the wrapper. Repeat with the remaining dough.

To fill the pot stickers, place about ½-tablespoon of the filling in the center of each wrapper. Avoid getting filling on the edges of the wrapper, which would prevent proper sealing. Fold each wrapper in half to form a half-moon shape. Seal the top center of each dumpling by pressing between the fingers and, starting at the center, make 3 pleats, working toward the bottom right. Repeat, working toward the bottom left corner. Press the dumplings down gently on the work surface to flatten the bottoms.

Heat a large non-stick skillet over high heat. Add the oil and swirl to coat. When the oil shimmers, add the pot stickers, flattened bottoms down, in rows of five, and cook in batches without disturbing until brown, about 6 minutes. Add about ½ cup of water and immediately cover to avoid splattering. Lift the cover and make sure about ⅛-inch of water remains in the pan; if not, add a bit more. Steam until the pot stickers are puffy yet firm and the water has evaporated, 6 to 8 minutes. If the water evaporates before the pot stickers are done, add more in ¼-cup increments. If the pot stickers seem done but water remains in the pan, drain it and return the pan to the stove top.

Continue to cook over high heat to allow the pot stickers to re-crisp on the bottom, 2 to 3 minutes. Transfer the pot stickers to a platter and serve with the dipping sauce in individual small bowls.

Serve with: *Heidler Grüner Veltleiner*

Crab is my favorite seafood and it's absolutely delicious combined with scallions, honey, and jicama. These raviolis are fried on each side to a crispy golden brown and the lemony dipping sauce with them is perfect.

CRISPY LEMON-CRAB RAVIOLIS

Makes 12 raviolis

½ pound Hot Water Dough, rolled out into thin 2- by 2-inch squares
1 pint picked crab meat
1 cup scallions, sliced and separated into white and green parts
1 cup jicama, ¼-inch dice
2 tablespoons honey
¼ cup olive oil
Juice and zest of 3 lemons
Kosher salt and freshly ground black pepper, to taste
Canola or grapeseed oil for cooking
Egg wash

In a bowl, mix together the crab, scallions, jicama, honey, 2 tablespoon of the olive oil, and juice of 1 lemon. Season with salt and pepper to taste. Lay out 6 wrappers, brush egg wash on the sides only (¼-inch), place a small mound of crab mixture in the middle, and top with second wrapper. Press firmly down on the edges to seal. Meanwhile, in a large sauté pan lightly coated with oil over medium-high heat, add the raviolis and brown on both sides. In the same hot pan, add the rest of the scallions and the zest, and deglaze with remaining lemon juice. Whisk in remaining olive oil, season and drizzle on top of raviolis when serving.

Serve with: *Heidler Grüner Veltleiner*

When most think of fried dough, they picture the golden puffs of dough covered in cinnamon sugar and butter sold at fairs and carnivals. Here is the savory version that is just as tasty: rounds of dough that are deep fried and then immediately sprinkled with salt and rubbed with garlic. My Auntie Susan Springer introduced me to this tasty snack: growing up, we would always visit her when we went to Michigan home games and she would prepare this as a snack. We could never get enough and I still can't!

FRIED DOUGH WITH GARLIC

½ pound of Hot Water Dough
1 tablespoon sugar
¼ cup scallion greens, sliced
1 head of garlic, split in half
Hawaiian sea salt

Mix the dough with the sugar and scallion greens. Portion into 8 equal pieces and stretch into thin ovals. Prepare a fryer at 375°F. Fry the dough until GB&D (golden brown & delicious) on both sides. Immediately season with salt, rub the garlic on it and serve.

Serve with: *Saison Dupont Vieille Provision*

Fans Meet Ming

MOM AND POP'S HSIEN BING (STUFFED BREAD)

Makes 8

This stuffed bread is actually more of a dumpling than bread, filled with a savory mixture of pork, mushrooms, garlic and ginger. Traditionally, it is served with raw garlic cloves but this is not for the faint of heart!

½ pound ground pork, chicken or turkey (or a mixture of all three)
2 cup mushrooms, chopped
1 garlic clove, finely chopped
1 tablespoon fresh ginger, finely chopped
1 scallion stalk, finely sliced
1 tablespoon sesame oil
2 tablespoons soy sauce
Kosher salt and freshly ground black pepper, to taste
½ pound Hot Water Dough

Mix first 8 ingredients well. Let mixture rest for 20 minutes. Roll hot water dough into 3-inch round skins, ¼-inch thick. Put one heaping tablespoon of mixed ingredients on one skin. Cover it with another skin. Press along the outer edges to form a closed pocket or "box". Immediately pan fry over low heat (high heat will burn) until golden brown on one side. Flip over to brown the other side.

Traditionally, these are served with vinegar to enhance taste as well as raw garlic cloves—a practice done when eating dumplings and noodles in North China. Be careful when biting into hot dumplings—like Shanghai soup dumpling, hot liquid may squirt out!

Serve with: *Saison Dupont Vieille Provision*

Hot sauces are popular around the world and I'm a huge fan of all of them: Latin salsas, Korean chile sauces, Indonesian sambals, and, my newest favorite, peri peri, a VERY hot chile paste I discovered in South Africa while there with lifestyle guru and consummate host Colin Cowie. I was so inspired by peri peri that I created this Kaffir Lime-Shallot Sambal. The aromatic citrus of the kaffir lime is spiked with heat, giving dishes from marinated grilled pork to rock lobsters a burst of sunny (and spicy) flavor that captures the essence of Thai cuisine.

KAFFIR LIME-SHALLOT SAMBAL

Makes 5 cups

- ¼ cup grapeseed oil
- 20 shallots, peeled and minced
- ¾ pound green jalapeños, stemmed, minced with the seeds
- 10 kaffir lime leaves, stemmed and minced
- ½ cup fresh lime juice
- 1 cup naturally brewed rice vinegar
- 1 cup sugar
- 1 teaspoon kosher salt

In a non-reactive sauce pan or wok over low heat, add the grapeseed oil, and sweat the shallots, chiles and kaffir lime leaves until soft, about 5 minutes. Add the lime juice, naturally brewed rice vinegar and sugar and bring slowly to a simmer. Reduce by 50 percent, about 20 to 30 minutes. Remove from heat and season with salt. Transfer to a food processor and pulse a few times. Let come to room temperature and transfer to a glass jar—it may be refrigerated for two weeks.

RECOMMENDED BEVERAGES

While in South Africa, I was given a tour of the beautiful Meerlust Estate by the incredibly friendly George Myburgh van Reenan and his charming auntie, Suzaan Hartze, the sister of proprietor Hannes Myburgh. I've chosen two from this particular vineyard to pair with the following dishes.

Meerlust Chardonnay

Where: Stellenbosch, South Africa
Grape: Chardonnay
Style: This is a full-bodied chardonnay with hints of preserved lemon, caramel, and roasted nuts. This is excellent with all types of seafood.

Meerlust Pinot Noir Reserve

Where: Stellenbosch, South Africa
Grape: Pinot Noir
Style: Features lush red and black berries, spices, and a hint of smoke but is balanced with vanilla oak and a lingering finish. This is great with "gamier" meats like duck and pork.

Whenever I'm in Jamaica, I always have the local specialty, jerk-style chicken and pork. In honor of that dish, I've paired my Kaffir Lime-Shallot Sambal with premium pork. I use the Porterhouse cut because cooking the meat with the bone-in means more flavor for pork as well as beef. The pork Porterhouse—especially the naturally fed from Niman Ranch—is fabulous.

MARINATED GRILLED PORK PORTERHOUSE WITH FRAGRANT RICE

Serves 4

4 naturally fed pork Porterhouse steaks, brined overnight in a "sweet sea water-tasting" liquid (very recommended, but not imperative)
1 cup Kaffir Lime-Shallot Sambal, plus 1 tablespoon for rice
3 cups basmati rice
Kosher salt and freshly ground black pepper, to taste

Rub the steaks with 1 cup of the Kaffir Lime-Shallot Sambal and let marinate at least 4 hours, preferably overnight. Prepare a hot clean grill, wiped with canola oil or sprayed with oil. Season the pork (lightly if brined) and grill both sides, about 6 to 8 minutes a side for medium. Let rest 5 minutes before slicing. Meanwhile, wash rice in cold tap water, 3 to 4 times, until water runs clear. Place in a rice cooker. Add 1 tablespoon of Kaffir Lime-Shallot Sambal and mix thoroughly. Season lightly with kosher salt and freshly ground black pepper to taste. Fill water to the first digit of your index finger as it touches the surface of the rice. Turn on cooker and you'll have perfect rice in 45 minutes. Place mound of rice on the plate. Slice the rested pork to the bone and lay on rice.

Serve with: *Meerlust Pinot Noir Reserve*

SIZZLING WHOLE MARINATED FARMED BASS

I love the texture and flavor frying provides and you can't beat the presentation of a whole fish— it's quite impressive. The tart-spicy sambal is a great condiment whose flavor accentuates the natural sweetness of the bass— delicious!

Serves 4

1 whole farmed hybrid bass (6 to 8 pounds) or the equivalent, eviscerated, scaled and scored
1½ cups Kaffir Lime-Shallot Sambal
2 cups rice flour
Grapeseed or peanut oil for frying
1 cup white wine
3 cups chicken stock
4 to 5 tablespoons butter, cubed and chilled
Kosher salt and freshly ground black pepper, to taste
2 scallions, sliced thinly on the bias, green parts only

Rub ½ cup Kaffir Lime-Shallot Sambal inside the fish and season inside and out with kosher salt and freshly ground black pepper to taste. Use 5-inch skewers at the opening so that it is tented. Dredge the entire fish in rice flour, shaking off excess. Fill a large roasting pan with 3 inches of oil and heat to 350 °F. Place fish in pan and cook for 5 minutes per side. A paring knife should easily penetrate the fish when done. Meanwhile, heat 1 to 2 tablespoons of oil in a heavy-bottomed sauce-pan over medium-high heat. Add 1 cup of Kaffir Lime-Shallot Sambal and sauté until hot. Deglaze pan with white wine and allow to reduce by 75 percent. Add the chicken stock, stir, and allow to reduce by 40 percent. Whisk in cold butter, stirring until smooth. Taste for seasoning. On a platter lined with banana leaves, place the fish, with skewers, "standing up" for dramatic presentation. Spoon pan sauce over the fish and garnish with scallion greens.

Serve with: *Chardonnay Meerlust Estate*

Rock Lobsters are a specialty of South Africa but you can always substitute New England lobsters with equally delicious results. This dish was prepared at the Mount Nelson Hotel in Capetown with Chef Stephen Templeton. The lobster tails are grilled with a compound butter flavored with the sambal. The result is an easy but decadent dish that has a smooth heat and burst of kaffir lime flavor—absolutely wonderful flavors with the buttery sweet lobster!

ROCK LOBSTER SMOTHERED IN KAFFIR LIME-SHALLOT BUTTER WITH TOASTED COCONUT RICE AND TOMATO SALAD

Serves 4

4 rock lobster tails, split
½ cup Kaffir Lime-Shallot Sambal
½ pound butter, room temperature
Kosher salt and freshly ground black pepper, to taste

2 cups steamed white rice
¼ cup toasted coconut

2 cups diced tomatoes, assorted varieties
Juice of 1 lemon
2 tablespoons extra virgin olive oil
Kosher salt and freshly ground black pepper, to taste

Season rock lobster tails with kosher salt and freshly ground black pepper to taste. Mix the butter and sambal and smother the seasoned tails with the compound butter. Grill or broil the tails for 6 to 8 minutes.

While the tails are cooking, make the coconut rice by tossing rice with toasted coconut and keep warm. In a medium-sized bowl, combine the tomatoes with the lemon juice and olive oil and season with kosher salt and freshly ground black pepper. Place a small amount of rice on plate and top with the lobster tail. Spoon tomato salad over tails and serve with extra Kaffir Lime-Shallot Sambal.

Serve with: *Meerlust Chardonnay*

COLIN COWIE'S FLASH SEARED SHRIMP WITH KAFFIR LIME-SHALLOT RAITA

Serves 2

Colin Cowie, my host during an amazing tour of South Africa, is the expert when it comes to entertaining with style. This dish does just what a party dish should do: it looks great, tastes fabulous, and will have people talking.

8 (approximately 1 pound) jumbo shrimp, peeled and deveined
3 tablespoons vegetable oil
¾ cup apples, peeled and grated
¾ cup red cabbage, finely shredded
¾ cup white cabbage, finely shredded
½ teaspoon salt
⅛ teaspoon freshly ground black pepper
Kaffir Lime-Shallot Raita (recipe follows)

Season shrimp with salt and pepper generously and set aside. Heat a medium skillet over high heat and add 2 tablespoons of vegetable oil. When hot, add apples, cabbage, salt and pepper and cook until soft but still crunchy, approximately 1 minute. Remove from pan and set aside.

Using the same skillet, add 1 tablespoon oil and place shrimp in single layer. Cook for 1 minute per side or until crisp. Lower the heat and continue cooking until done (approximately 3 to 5 minutes).

To serve, divide the cabbage and apple slaw evenly among large dinner plates, placing the slaw in the center of the plate. Place 4 shrimp on top of the slaw, drizzle with Kaffir Raita and serve immediately.

Serve with: *Chardonnay Meerlust Estate*

KAFFIR LIME-SHALLOT RAITA
1 cup non fat Greek yogurt
3 tablespoons mint
2 tablespoons Kaffir Lime-Shallot Sambal

Place all ingredients in a blender and purée until smooth.

*Colin Cowie's Flash Seared Shrimp
with Kaffir Lime-Shallot Raita*

49

Many meals in Chinese restaurants end with a dessert of lychees—the perfumed exotic fruit really tastes like nothing else. While sweet, they are fantastic in savory dishes when paired with mangoes and spicy jalapeño peppers as done in this purée, adding an incomparable fresh and tropical sweet heat to a variety of dishes.

LYCHEE-MANGO PURÉE

Makes 4 cups

- 1 large yellow onion, sliced
- 1 tablespoon minced ginger
- 2 jalapeños, stemmed, minced with the seeds
- 4 ripe mangoes, peeled and roughly chopped
- 1 cup whole peeled lychees, roughly chopped (preferably fresh, but canned is fine as long as they are whole and well drained)
- Juice of 2 limes
- ⅓ cup grapeseed oil plus some to cook with
- Kosher salt and freshly ground black pepper, to taste

In a sauté pan coated lightly with oil over high heat, sauté the onions, ginger and jalapeños until soft, about 4 minutes. Season with kosher salt and freshly ground black pepper to taste. Add the mangoes and lychees and cook for only 3 minutes until hot. Transfer to a blender and purée at a high speed in batches. Add the lime juice and drizzle in the oil to emulsify. Check again for flavor. Store in a glass jar, covered, in the fridge for two weeks.

RECOMMENDED BEVERAGES

Pascal Bourgogne Blanc

Where: Puligny Montrachet, Burgundy, France
Grape: Chardonnay
Style: This chardonnay is neither heavy nor oaky and instead features more mineral qualities. Produced in the revered village of Puligny Montrachet in the Burgundy region, this is a taste of an exclusive Burgundy wine at a very reasonable price.

Harpoon "UFO" Hefweizen

Where: Boston, Massachusetts
Style: "Hefweizen" means wheat beer and this one features the aroma of tropical fruits and bananas and is slightly sweet but still crisp. Fermentation occurs at a slightly higher temperature and it is bottled without being filtered which produces a fuller flavor. This beer is best when served with a lemon, the citrus cutting through the rich flavor of the beer.

I first had lobster and mango together in the Caribbean and loved the sweet, slightly acidic mango with the sweet, rich lobster meat. Here, a special lunchtime favorite, lobster salad, gets a burst of flavor with the addition of Lychee-Mango Purée, sweet crunchy jicama, and scallions, creating a colorful and tasty lobster salad that may make you forget the more staid original.

LYCHEE-MANGO LOBSTER SALAD

Serves 4

3 1½-pound lobsters, steamed, meat out of the shell and cut into bite size pieces, claws whole
1 large jicama, peeled and cut into ½-inch dice
4 each scallions, sliced, save 2 tablespoons sliced scallion greens for garnish
½ cup Lychee-Mango Purée, plus 4 tablespoons for garnish
2 heads butter lettuce leaves separated, washed and dried
Kosher salt and freshly ground black pepper, to taste

In a large bowl, mix together the lobster meat, jicama, scallions, and Lychee-Mango Purée. Season with kosher salt and freshly ground black pepper to taste. On salad plates, lay out 3 leaves of butter lettuce and top with small mound of lobster salad. Drizzle puree on top for garnish.

Serve with: *Pascal Bourgogne Blanc*

Orchids on the Set

Scallops wrapped in bacon are the now retro and ubiquitous appetizers that always seem to surface at wedding receptions—but people never seem to tire of the sweet scallop and salty bacon combo because it's so good. I've taken those great flavors and added them to another favorite—fried rice—though I've substituted orzo for rice to jazz it up. I then drizzle the dish generously with the Purée, its sweetness bringing out the sweetness of the plump scallops.

SCALLOP AND BACON FRIED ORZO WITH LYCHEE-MANGO PUREE

Serves 4

½ pound sliced bacon
2 eggs, lightly beaten
1 red onion, cut into ¼-inch dice
1 pound small scallops, prepped (U-30's)
½ pound orzo, blanched
2 tablespoons cilantro, chopped, plus 4 sprigs for garnish
½ cup Lychee-Mango Purée
Grapeseed or canola oil for cooking
Kosher salt and freshly ground black pepper, to taste

In a large non-stick sauté pan over medium heat, render the bacon until cooked through and crisp, about 10 minutes. Transfer bacon to a plate lined with paper towels and when cooled, chop up. Return the pan to the stove and over high heat, add the eggs and scramble soft. Transfer eggs to a plate. In same pan over high heat, add 1 tablespoon of oil and sauté the onions until soft, about 3 minutes. Add the scallops, sauté for 1 minute, then add orzo, cilantro, bacon, and eggs. Heat thoroughly and season with kosher salt and freshly ground black pepper to taste. Using a rice bowl or ramekin, mold the fried orzo and turn upside on plates. Generously drizzle the Purée on the plate and orzo.

Serve with: *Pascal Bourgogne Blanc*

*Scallop and Bacon Fried Orzo
with Lychee-Mango Purée*

When I moved to Chicago after graduation, a great friend, Chicago-bred Eric Siegel, drove me from Cornell directly to Gold Coast Hot Dogs. It was my first introduction to genuine Chicago Dogs and I was hooked. Here is my tribute, done in the East-West way.

'CHICAGO DOG' WITH LYCHEE-MANGO-CORN RELISH

Serves 4

3 ears of corn, boiled in salted water, taken off of the cob, cooled
1 cup Lychee-Mango Purée
4 natural beef hot dogs (such as Niman Ranch)
4 poppy seed buns, steamed
4 pickle spears
2 small tomatoes, cut into 8 wedges
For garnish: Dijon mustard, celery salt, little pickled chiles and bright green relish for show

In a small bowl, mix together the corn and purée and season with kosher salt and freshly ground black pepper to taste. Boil the dogs and steam the buns. Spread the mustard on the bun, then place the dog. Top with relish, pickles, tomato slices and celery salt. Never ketchup!

Serve with: Harpoon "UFO" Hefweizen—a beer is a must with a dog!

'Chicago Dog' with Lychee-Mango-Corn Relish   57

TODD ENGLISH'S BROCHETTE OF DUCK WITH LYCHEE, MANGO, AND FENNEL SLAW

By now, it's hard to find anyone that hasn't heard of über-chef (and great friend) Todd English—his restaurant empire, which began in Boston, now spans the world. Here he has flavored an awesome fennel slaw with the Lychee-Mango Purée and served it with skewers of petite duck, chorizo, cipollini—a mild Italian onion—and fingerling potatoes, presenting a myriad of wonderful flavors in every little bite.

Serves 4

8 ounces chorizo, cooked
8 ounces duck breast, cut into 1-ounce cubes
8 cipollini, blanched
8 fingerling potatoes, small and cooked
Marinade (recipe follows)
Fennel Slaw (recipe follows)
For garnish: Lychee-Mango Puree and whole cilantro sprigs

With a metal or soaked wood skewer, thread the first four ingredients in an alternating fashion. Place in marinade and cover for several hours. While marinating, make the fennel slaw.

When ready, heat the grill, season brochettes with salt and pepper, and grill for 3 minutes on each side. Place fennel slaw in the middle of the plate and top with a grilled brochette. Drizzle with Lychee-Mango Purée and garnish with whole cilantro sprigs.

Serve with: *Harpoon "UFO" Hefweizen*

MARINADE

¼ cup honey
2 teaspoons allspice
Zest of 1 orange
½ cup balsamic vinegar

¼ cup sesame oil
¾ cup extra virgin olive oil
2 tablespoons fennel seed, cracked
3 tablespoons chopped cilantro

In a blender, combine first four ingredients. Start blender and slowly drizzle in the oils. Remove from blender and mix with cilantro and fennel seed.

FENNEL SLAW

2 bulbs fennel
¾ cup Lychee-Mango Purée
3 tablespoons extra virgin olive oil
3 tablespoons cilantro, chopped
3 tablespoons scallions, chopped

With a Japanese mandolin, slice fennel as thinly as possible. Toss with remaining ingredients and season with salt and pepper.

MASTER RECIPE

*The first time I ever had shallots
and miso together was at Nobu—they
had been combined in a simple salad and I
was hooked. Inspired by that amazing
flavor combination, I created my
own Miso-Shallot Vinaigrette.*

MISO-SHALLOT VINAIGRETTE

Makes 5½ cups

- 1 cup shiro miso
- 1 cup shallots, sliced
- 1 teaspoon togarashi or chile pepper
- 1 tablespoon sugar
- Juice of 2 lemons
- ½ cup naturally brewed rice vinegar
- 1 teaspoon sesame oil
- 3 cups grapeseed or canola oil
- Kosher salt and freshly ground black pepper, to taste

In a blender, add the miso, shallots, togarashi, sugar, lemon juice, naturally brewed rice vinegar and sesame oil and blend together at a high speed until smooth. Drizzle the oil slowly into the blender to emulsify. Check for seasoning. Store in a covered glass jar and place in the fridge for up to two weeks.

RECOMMENDED BEVERAGES

Note: *For this master, I've selected two wines from the Burgundy region of France, a white and a red, that are excellent village wines. Both are half bottles, which is perfect when cooking for two. They allow for sampling a variety of wines with different dishes and courses without opening entire bottles of wine. This also lowers the price point, allowing for more affordable sampling of expensive wines.*

Jean-Marc Pillot Chassagne-Montrachet

Where: Burgundy, France
Grape: Chardonnay
Style: This is a richer chardonnay that features a light oak quality with none of standard butteriness. It balances well with sushi and lighter food, but still has the backbone for richer dishes such as chicken and pork.

Domaine du Jacques Geverey-Chambertin

Where : Burgundy, France
Grape: Pinot Noir
Style: This is a lighter-bodied pinot noir that has notes of bing cherries and the earth. It is excellent with lamb, but is still delicate enough for lighter chicken dishes.

Salmon and miso are a match made in heaven—the salty fermented flavor of miso pairs so perfectly with the rich seafood and provides a dose of Umami— that fifth taste discovered by a Japanese professor—which translates loosely to "savory" or "meaty".

SEARED SESAME-CRUSTED RARE SALMON WITH MIZUNA SALAD

Serves 4

1 pound wild salmon, skinned and cut into 4-ounce pieces
¼ cup untoasted sesame seeds
½ cup Miso-Shallot Vinaigrette
½ pound mizuna greens, washed and spun very dry
½ pint cherry tomatoes, cut in half
Kosher salt and freshly ground black pepper, to taste

Season the salmon with kosher salt and freshly ground black pepper. Place the sesame seeds on a plate and spread out so that 50 percent of the plate is covered with sesame seeds and press the salmon in the seeds. In a sauté pan coated lightly with oil over high heat, sear the salmon for only 1 to 2 minutes per side until sesame seeds are toasted. The salmon will still be rare and cool in the middle. Slice the salmon into ¼-inch thin slices. In a large bowl, toss the vinaigrette with the mizuna and tomatoes. Plate a pile of salad and top with the salmon slices.

Serve with: *Jean-Marc Pillot Chassagne-Montrachet*

Garlic and lamb are a classic combination popular in Provence and all over Greece. Shallots are the softer, milder version of garlic but provide great flavor just the same. The potatoes and carrots are cooked along with the meat, absorbing the wonderful flavors and making this an easy one-dish meal.

MARINATED LAMB WITH ROASTED YUKON GOLD POTATOES AND CARROTS

Serves 4

2 naturally fed lamb racks
1½ cups Miso-Shallot Vinaigrette
3 large Yukon gold potatoes, skin on, washed and cut into 1-inch cubes
1 pound carrots nubs, peeled
1 cup scallions sliced, white and green parts separated
Kosher salt and freshly ground black pepper, to taste

In a pan or dish large enough for the 2 lamb racks, rub 1 cup of the vinaigrette all over the lamb and let marinate for 4 hours. Preheat an oven to 525°F (use convection if available) and place a roasting pan in the oven to heat. Toss the potatoes, carrots and scallion greens with remaining vinaigrette and season with kosher salt and freshly ground black pepper to taste. Open oven, pull out rack and pour mixture into pan. There will be a good sizzle. Season the lamb rack with kosher salt and freshly ground black pepper to taste and place on top of mixture. Close oven and roast until lamb is brown, about 15 to 20 minutes. Lower the oven to 250 and roast for an additional 10 minutes. Stick a paring knife in to check for the temperature you want: hot is medium-well, warm is medium, warm-cool is medium-rare, cool is rare. Let rest 8 minutes on a board before slicing rack into chops. Remove the potato-carrot mixture and place on a large platter. Top with lamb chops.

Serve with: *Domaine du Jacques Geverey-Chambertin*

Marinated Lamb with Roasted Yukon Gold Potatoes and Carrots

MARINATED GRILLED VEGETABLE HAND ROLLS

Serves 4

1 Japanese eggplant, cut into long ½-inch slices
1 red onion, cut into ½-inch slices
1 red bell pepper, roasted and peeled, cut into slices
1 zucchini, cut into long ½-inch slices
1 portobello, stemmed
1 cup Miso-Shallot Vinaigrette
4 cups steamed Koshi Hikari sushi rice
1 package toasted nori sheets
Kosher salt and freshly ground black pepper, to taste

In a large bowl, mix the veggies with the marinade. Season with kosher salt and freshly ground black pepper to taste. Prepare a hot clean grill, wiped or sprayed with canola oil. Grill the veggies until soft and colored. Set aside. Place a sheet of the nori on a work surface, shiny side down. Spread about ½-cup of the rice onto the lower half of the nori, patting it down lightly. Top with a small amount of grilled vegetables, placing them diagonally across the rice from the upper left corner to the bottom right, then fold the lower left-hand corner of the nori toward the right side to enclose the filling. Continue to roll toward the nori's left side to form a cone. Repeat with the remaining nori, rice, and filling. Serve immediately.

Serve with: *Jean-Marc Pillot Chassagne-Montrachet* or *Domaine du Jacques Geverey-Chambertin*

MICHAEL SCHLOW'S POTATO-CRUSTED HALIBUT WITH WILD MUSHROOMS AND MISO-SHALLOT VINAIGRETTE

Michael Schlow is an unbelievable chef, who has three awesome restaurants in Boston, and an even better friend. I always love seeing what Michael will do with my master sauce. Here he's taken halibut and coated it with, of all things, dehydrated potato flakes—also known as instant mashed potatoes! But this gourmet chef knows what he's doing because the coating becomes golden and crispy. Served with a sauté of wild mushrooms, fresh thyme, and Miso-Shallot Vinaigrette, this is an elegant and tasty dish. You may find Michael in Boston at either Radius, Via Matta, or Great Bay.

Serves 2

2 6-ounce pieces of halibut, 2-inches thick, squared
1 egg
1 ounce water
1 cup all natural dehydrated potato flakes
2 pinches fresh thyme
2 ounces canola oil
1 cup assorted wild mushrooms, preferably morels
1 ounce extra virgin olive oil
Kosher salt and freshly ground black pepper, to taste
3 tablespoons of Miso-Shallot Vinaigrette

Whisk the egg with water in a small bowl and season to taste. In another small bowl, add one pinch of fresh thyme to the potato flakes. Season the flesh side of the fish with salt and pepper and dip the seasoned side into the egg wash, allowing excess to drip off. Dip that side into the potato flakes and press gently (you will only be coating one side). Place the canola oil in a sauté pan and place the fish, crust side down, into the cold pan and place over high heat. Cook for approximately 4 minutes, the crust should start to turn a nice golden brown. Season the other side of the fish before flipping, reduce the heat to medium and finish cooking, another 4 minutes. While the fish is cooking, prepare the mushrooms. In a sauté pan, over high heat, add the olive oil and the mushrooms and sauté for another 2 to 3 minutes, adding the remaining thyme and one tablespoon of the Vinaigrette. Season with salt and pepper. To serve, divide the mushrooms onto the center of the two dinner plates. Place the fish, crust side up on top of the mushrooms and spoon some of the vinaigrette around the mushrooms and the fish in a decorative pattern.

Serve with: *Domaine du Jacques Geverey-Chambertin*

MASTER RECIPE

*Citrus is used in both Eastern
and Western cuisines: It has the ability
to both brighten flavors and balance richness.
This master combines the familiar orange
with the Japanese yuzu, a very sour
Japanese citrus fruit. This syrup
works for beef, seafood, and
poultry dishes.*

ORANGE-YUZU SYRUP

Makes 3 pints

> 3 pints freshly squeezed orange juice
> 1 pint freshly squeezed lemon juice
> 1 pint mirin
> ¾ pint yuzu
> ½ to ¾ pint grapeseed or canola oil
> Kosher salt to taste

In a non-reactive sauce pan over low heat, add orange juice, lemon juice and mirin and reduce slowly by 70 percent. Transfer to a blender and on high speed add the yuzu, then drizzle in the oil. Season with salt and check for flavor. Transfer to a glass jar, and when cooled, seal with lid and store in fridge for up to two weeks.

RECOMMENDED BEVERAGES

Outouka Junmai Premium Sake

Where: Okayama, Japan
Style: Sakes are Japanese rice wines and this one is dry, crisp, and herby, which helps to balance the sweetness of the syrup. The hint of cherry blossoms allows it to bond with fruit-based flavors in these dishes using the Orange-Yuzu syrup. It is best to serve this sake cold.

Protocolo Rosé

Where: Castilla, Spain
Grape: Temparnillo
Style: This is a dry, rich, pink wine with flavors and aromas of raspberries, strawberries, and rose petals. It is very crisp and refreshing, wonderful with Asian food and in the hot summer months.

I grew up eating orange beef and yuzu seemed to be a natural source for citrus in this dish. The tart yuzu cuts some of the orange's sweetness and the beef's richness.

WOK-STIRRED ORANGE-YUZU BEEF

Serves 4

1 tablespoon minced garlic
1 tablespoon minced ginger
1 bunch scallions, cut into 2-inch pieces
1½ pounds naturally fed hanger steak, sliced against the grain, ¼-inch thick slices
½ cup Orange-Yuzu Syrup plus 2 tablespoons for garnish
Grapeseed or canola oil for cooking
Kosher salt and freshly ground black pepper, to taste
Steamed rice

In a wok (preferably non-stick) or sauté pan coated lightly with oil over high heat, add the garlic and ginger and sauté until fragrant, about 1 to 2 minutes. Add the beef and season with kosher salt and freshly ground black pepper to taste. Wok stir for 2 minutes until beef is cooked medium. Add the syrup and the scallion greens, check again for flavor, and place on a serving platter, drizzling with the remaining syrup. Serve with steamed rice.

Serve with: *Protocolo Rosé*

The Chinese make a traditional dish of thickly battered fried shrimp with mayonnaise and walnuts. I love fried food as much as the next guy but I wanted to lighten the dish up. I instead coat the shrimp with panko and serve them with the citrusy Orange-Yuzu Syrup and greens. This version is definitely not as heavy but still very good!

CRISPY BUTTERFLIED SHRIMP WITH ORANGE-YUZU SYRUP

Serves 4

12 jumbo shrimp, peeled and cleaned, full butterfly, tail on
1 cup all-purpose flour, lightly seasoned with kosher salt and freshly ground black pepper
4 eggs, beaten
2 cups panko or other fine bread crumbs
2 tablespoons chives, chopped
½ cup Orange-Yuzu Syrup
2 cups mesclun
Juice of one lemon
Kosher salt and freshly ground black pepper, to taste
Grapeseed or canola oil for cooking

Flatten each shrimp by hand and lightly dredge in flour, followed by egg, and then panko. In a sauce pan coated lightly with ¼-inch of oil over medium-high heat, add the shrimp and shallow fry each side until golden brown, about 2 minutes a side. Transfer to a plate lined with paper towels. In a large bowl, lightly toss the mesclun with the juice of one lemon and season with kosher salt and freshly ground black pepper to taste. On each of 4 plates, place a small mound of mesclun surrounded by 3 crispy shrimp. Generously drizzle with syrup.

Serve with: *Outouka Junmai Premium Sake*

Serving a whole anything always makes for a gorgeous presentation and this glazed chicken on a platter of wild rice salad not only looks great but tastes great too. Two dishes I love, duck à l'orange and Mediterranean-style lemon chicken, were the inspiration for this dish. The tart-sweet glaze produces a deeply golden bird while the earthy wild rice and crisp haricots verts are dressed in a vinaigrette made with Orange-Yuzu Syrup, savory shallots, and smooth Dijon, providing the perfect complement. This dish is tart, sweet, and savory all at once and is great for a crowd.

ORANGE GLAZED CHICKEN WITH WILD RICE SALAD

Serves 4 to 6

1 whole 6-pound organic, naturally-fed or kosher chicken, washed and patted dry
1 cup Orange-Yuzu Syrup plus 2 tablespoons for garnish
2 shallots, minced
1 tablespoon Dijon mustard
2 tablespoons naturally brewed rice vinegar
2 tablespoons grapeseed oil
½ pound haricot verts, blanched in salted water, shocked in ice water, cut into 1-inch pieces
3 cups cooked wild rice
Kosher salt and freshly ground black pepper, to taste

Preheat an oven to 500°F. Season the chicken well, inside and out. Rub half of the syrup all over the chicken. Place in a hot oven and cook until brown (may need to rotate), about 15 minutes. Place a foil tent on chicken and reduce oven to 325°F and roast chicken until legs move easily when jiggled or paring knife comes out hot at the leg joint, about an additional 40 to 45 minutes. Meanwhile, in a small bowl, whisk together the shallots, Dijon mustard, and remaining ½ cup Orange-Yuzu Syrup. Season with kosher salt and freshly ground black pepper to taste. Toss the rice and haricot verts with the vinaigrette and check for flavor. Transfer chicken to a cutting board and let rest for at least 5 minutes. Carve the chicken into pieces and serve family style on top of a bed of the rice salad.

Serve with: *Protocolo Rosé*

HIROKO SHIMBO'S TATSUTA PORK SALAD WITH ORANGE-YUZU SYRUP

Serves 2

Hiroko Shimbo is a brilliant Japanese chef who is also a cookbook author and chef instructor in New York City and I was psyched to have her use the Orange-Yuzu Syrup to create a Tatsuta Pork Salad. Tatsuta is a popular Japanese technique where meat or poultry is marinated in a ginger mixture, dredged in a starch, and then deep fried. The fried pork is light and crispy and quite tasty tossed with peppery arugula, purple endive, asparagus and of course, the sweet-tart Orange-Yuzu Syrup.

1 7-ounce bone-removed pork chop, cut into 10 slices
2 teaspoons ginger juice
2 cloves garlic, finely grated
1½ tablespoons shoyu (soy sauce)
10 stalks asparagus, blanched and cut into quarter portions
1 large purple endive, cut into strips, slanted
1 cup baby arugula
Olive oil or canola oil for cooking and tossing the salad
Potato starch
⅓ cup Orange-Yuzu Syrup

In a bowl combine the ginger juice, grated garlic, shoyu and 2 tablespoons of the Orange-Yuzu Syrup. Marinate the sliced pork for 10 minutes. Remove pork from the marinade and wipe it with a paper towel. Dredge slices in the potato starch and shake off excess, then place between two pieces of plastic and pound thin. Sprinkle with more potato starch and repeat pounding. Dredge slices in potato starch again and place in a pan with a shallow layer of oil that has been heated to 275°F. Cook until the outsides are golden and the strips are cooked through. In a bowl combine the asparagus, endive and arugula and toss with a little olive oil and salt. Add the Orange-Yuzu Syrup and toss again. Serve the salad with the pork

Serve with: *Outouka Junmai Premium Sake*

MASTER RECIPE

*Many think of America as
the great melting pot but when
it comes to international flavors, it's very
hard to beat Singapore, the Grand Central
Station of Asian, Indian, and Western foods.
But, since a trip to Singapore may not be in
most people's immediate plans, I've included
this recipe for Red Rendang—a curry paste
that can be used on everything from beef to
seafood to poultry. It packs a lot of flavor
and is probably unlike anything you've
ever tasted. I love spicy food and this is
really hot—if you would like to make
it more mild, simply decrease the
amount of chiles.*

RED RENDANG

Makes 5 cups

½ cup dried Thai bird chiles

1 cup chopped lemongrass, white part only

2 cups sliced shallots

1 bunch cilantro, stemmed (save the stems), leaves washed and spun dry

½ cup lime juice

½ cup fish sauce

½ cup paprika

2 tablespoons cumin, toasted and ground

2 tablespoons coriander, toasted and ground

¼ cup grapeseed oil

Kosher salt, to taste

In a food processor, combine the chiles, lemongrass, shallots, and the leaves and 6 stems of cilantro and blend until a rough purée is formed. Do not over-blend to a smooth paste. Add the lime juice, fish sauce and dried spices. Drizzle in the oil, blending on a low speed, and check for seasoning. Transfer to a glass jar, and when cooled, seal with lid and store in fridge for up to two weeks.

RECOMMENDED BEVERAGES

Terlaner Classico

Where: Tyrol, Italy
Grape: blend of Pinot Bianco, Chardonnay, Sauvignon Blanc
Style: This wine is a blend of three grapes grown in the "classico" district of "Terlano", whose soil is rich in minerals, and is a blend that has been successively made for over 100 years. It is a harmonious taste that is quite strong on the palate.

Charles Milton Rosé

Where: Barossa, Australia
Grape: blend of Grenache, Cabernet Sauvignon, Pinot Meunier
Style: In addition to this aromatic blend, small amounts of shiraz and reisling are blended to add a touch of spice and tannin. This wine should be served chilled.

One of the most delicious dishes I ever had in Singapore was a chile skate. Instead of skate, I've substituted salmon and added cooling sweet mango to balance the spicy richness of the Rendang. Steaming in a banana leaf not only looks beautiful on the plate and imparts a subtle exotic flavor, but even more importantly, guarantees a wonderfully moist fish.

BANANA LEAF-WRAPPED INDONESIAN SALMON

Serves 4

4 pieces salmon fillet, 6 ounces each, skin off
½ cup Red Rendang
2 cups cooked basmati rice
2 mangoes, peeled and cut into ½-inch dice
1 banana leaf, cut into four 12- x 12-inch sheets
2 limes
Kosher salt and freshly ground black pepper, to taste

Set up a large steamer with boiling water. Marinate the salmon in the Red Rendang for 1 hour on both sides. On each banana leaf, place a small mound of rice topped with mango, squeeze some lime juice on top, and season with salt and pepper. Place salmon on top, cover with a bit more Red Rendang, and envelop the salmon with the banana leaf so that the packet opens with the fish on top. Place packet in steamer and cook for 8 to 10 minutes. Serve in the package on a plate.

Serve with: *Terlaner Classico*

SOUTH EAST ASIAN LAMB STEW

Lamb stew is usually thought of as an Anglo-Saxon comfort food. Here, lamb is seasoned with the exotic Red Rendang. This stew is proof of how tasty this curry paste is with meat and how flavor-packed a "homey" lamb stew can be.

Serves 4 to 6

2 pounds lamb stew meat, cut into 1-inch dice
½ cup Red Rendang
1 pound button mushrooms, stemmed, halved
1 pound carrot nubs
4 cups cooked couscous
Canola or grapeseed oil to coat
Kosher salt and freshly ground black pepper, to taste

Season the lamb with salt and pepper. In a stock pot coated lightly with oil over high heat, brown the meat then set aside. In the same pot, add the Red Rendang and stir. Add the mushrooms and carrots and return the meat to the pot and cover with water. Season with salt and pepper and check for flavor. Bring to a simmer and cook until meat is tender, about 1½ hours. Serve on top of warm couscous.

Serve with: *Charles Milton Rosé*

Enjoying his 'job'

Here is the Southeast Asian version of surf and turf. Spicy ground pork and calamari are sautéed with crunchy and slightly sweet jicama and served on steamed jasmine rice.

SAUTÉED CALAMARI AND PORK

Serves 4

1 pound naturally fed ground pork
½ cup Red Rendang
2 cups jicama, cut into ½-inch dice
1 pound calamari (3- to 5-inch tubes,) cut into ½-inch rings and large tentacles sliced
Steamed jasmine rice
Canola or grapeseed oil for cooking

In a stock pot, coated lightly with oil on high heat, brown the pork, then add the Red Rendang and stir. Add the jicama and heat through, about 3 minutes, and then, still over high heat, add the calamari and quickly sauté, about 1 minute. Season, check for flavor, and serve with steamed rice.

Serve with: *Terlaner Classico*

Ming, chef Susur Lee, and Susur's kids, Kai & Levi

SUSUR LEE'S LAMB CHOPS WITH MANGO AND FRESH MINT

Serves 4 as an appetizer

I consider my friend Susur Lee, not only one of the best chefs in the world, but also a mentor. He is a master of East/West cuisine and familiar with this curry paste from Singapore. Deluxe lamb chops are baked with a coating of Red Rendang mixed with fresh bread-crumbs and cilantro and served with a cool mint sauce on slices of sweet mango. This dish is an explosion of amazing flavors, colors, and textures, but, then again, I wouldn't expect anything less from a master like him. If you find yourself in Toronto, you must visit him at his restaurants: Susur's and his new joint right next door, Lee's.

4 lamb chops
1 tablespoon Red Rendang
1 egg yolk
1 tablespoon fresh breadcrumbs
1½ teaspoons minced cilantro

1 mango, peeled and sliced into thin ovals
Mint sauce (recipe follows)

Place a tray or pan in oven and preheat to 450°F. Meanwhile, in a small bowl mix the Red Rendang, egg yolk, fresh breadcrumbs, and cilantro. Make a quarter-sized ball of this mixture and place on each lamb chop. Carefully remove heated pan from oven, spray with non-stick spray, place lamb chops on it, and put back in the oven for 8 minutes.

While lamb chops are in the oven, make the mint sauce by placing all ingredients in a blender and puréeing until smooth. To serve, place a mango oval on the plate, top with a lamb chop, and drizzle with mint sauce.

Serve with: *Charles Milton Rosé*

MINT SAUCE

2 tablespoons sugar
Juice of one lemon
1 cup mint leaves
1 tablespoon cilantro, minced
Pinch of salt
2 Thai bird chiles
2 tablespoons water

MASTER RECIPE

The aroma of simmering
Red Roast is one of the most
vivid smells from my childhood, next
to ginger and garlic. The mixture of sweet rock
candy, spicy ginger, chiles, and wine would per-
fume and warm the house like nothing else. It
is, at once, sweet, salty, and spicy, imparting
all these flavors to a duck or pork shoulder
that is braised to sublime tenderness.
THIS is comfort food!

RED ROAST BRAISING LIQUID

Makes 7 to 8 Cups

- *1 quart soy sauce*
- *2 cups red wine*
- *1 cup balsamic vinegar*
- *2 cups water*
- *2 pounds rock candy or brown sugar*
- *1 large ginger root, washed, cut into long ¼-inch slices*
- *3 dried Thai bird chiles*
- *1 head of garlic, split*
- *1 star anise*
- *1 bunch scallions, cut into 3-inch lengths*
- *1 orange, quartered*
- *3 large pieces of orange rind*
- *2 cinnamon sticks*

In a non-reactive stock pot, add all ingredients and bring to a simmer until the rock candy melts. Let simmer until reduced by 25 percent, about 1 hour, then strain. Let cool to room temperature. Store in a glass jar in the fridge for up to 2 weeks.

RECOMMENDED BEVERAGES

Catena Malbec

Where: Mendoza, Argentina
Grape: Malbec
Style: Malbec is one of the lesser known Bordeaux grapes but is gaining popularity in South America. It is a rich, dark, tannic wine that has plum and black currant notes. It is fantastic with slow cooked, braised, and barbecued meats, making it a natural pairing for many of these dishes.

Newton Claret

Where: Sonoma, California
Grape: Merlot, with small amounts of Cabernet Franc and Cabernet Sauvignon
Style: Claret is the British term for Bordeaux wines. This one features flavors of blueberries and coffee and has richer flavors but a lighter body than Malbec, making it very accessible to a wide range of dishes.

Traditionally, the Chinese braise an entire duck in the Red Roast liquid but it can be difficult to remove it whole from the sauce. This recipe simplifies things by using only duck legs, which are really the best part of the duck anyway.

RED ROAST DUCK LEGS WITH SWEET POTATOES AND DAIKON

Serves 4

10 duck legs
2 to 4 cups Red Roast Braising Liquid, to cover
1 large sweet potato, peeled, cut into ½-inch rounds
1 large daikon, peeled, cut into ½-inch rounds
Serve with hot brown rice

In a non-reactive stock pot, place the duck legs and cover with braising liquid. Bring to a simmer and cook legs for 1½ to 2 hours, periodically skimming rendered duck fat and reserving for future use, until the meat is just falling off of the bone. For the last 20 minutes, add the sweet potatoes and daikon. In large pasta bowls, lay out the slices of vegetables in an alternating pattern like 'carpaccio'. Place a small mound of rice on top, and then 2 duck legs. Ladle enough liquid to cover the 'carpaccio'.

Serve with: *Catena Malbec*

We serve butterfish here at Blue Ginger as a substitute for the over-fished Chilean sea bass. It has a rich, unctuous flavor that is incredibly tasty when braised with snow cabbage in the salty, sweet, and spicy braising liquid.

LIGHTLY BRAISED BUTTERFISH WITH SNOW CABBAGE

Serves 4

4 pieces butterfish fillet, skin off, 6 to 8 ounces each
2 cups Red Roast Braising Liquid, to reach half way up the fish in pan
1 medium head of Snow Cabbage (Napa), cut into ½-inch strips
1 tablespoon pink peppercorns to garnish

In a large non-reactive sauce pan with cover, place a bed of cabbage and top with the fish. Pour braising liquid to cover the cabbage and cover the fish halfway. Cover and slowly bring to a simmer. Cook for 10 to 12 minutes until the fish is done and a knife easily pierces the flesh. Carefully remove the cabbage and fish together, one piece at a time with a fish spatula or spatula with holes directly to a soup plate. Garnish with pink peppercorns.

Serve with: *Newton Claret*

The best way to make this is to use the leftover braising liquid from the duck recipe—that will add lots of flavor—but you may use a new recipe of Red Roast Braising Liquid as well with great results. The liquid is reduced and puréed with carrots and butter resulting in a sweet, rich syrup that is absolutely amazing with rib eye steaks—the most flavorful cut of beef, in my opinion.

GRILLED RIB EYE STEAK WITH RED ROAST-CARROT SYRUP

Serves 4

3 cups Red Roast Braising Liquid, preferably reserved from duck recipe
1 pound carrot nubs
½ cup water
4 tablespoons butter, cut into cubes and chilled
2 large naturally fed rib eye steaks
2 cups baby spinach
2 tablespoons chopped chives
Kosher salt and freshly ground black pepper, to taste

Prepare a hot grill, cleaned and wiped or sprayed with canola oil. In a medium non-reactive sauce pan add the carrots and braising liquid and bring to a simmer. Cook until carrots are done, about 20 minutes. Remove carrots and keep reducing the liquid until a maple syrup consistency is achieved when spooned on a chilled plate. Add back the carrots and check for flavor. Pour carrots and reduced liquid into the blender and purée, adding enough water to thin it to a thick sauce consistency. Add butter in cubes and purée until smooth, checking for seasoning. Meanwhile, season the steaks with salt and lots of pepper. Grill the steaks for 10 to 12 minutes for medium rare. Let rest 5 minutes before slicing. On a large platter, plate the baby spinach, top with slices of beef and drizzle remaining syrup. Garnish with chives.

Serve with: *Catena Malbec*

MOM AND POP'S RED ROAST SHANK SANDWICHES

Makes 4 sandwiches

2 pieces of beef shank (about 2 pounds total)
1 quart Red Roast Braising Liquid
White country loaf, sliced
1 tomato, sliced
Lettuce, shredded

Anyone who loves pot roast or brisket, will adore this Red Roast Shank. A beef shank is left to cook for a few hours and the result is meltingly tender beef that has been infused with all the flavors of the braising liquid. Left in the fridge overnight, the flavors develop even more. This makes ridiculously good sandwiches!

In a nonstick 6 to 8 quart size pot, brown all sides of the beef shank in a ½-inch of vegetable oil; the process takes about 10 minutes. Add Red Roast Braising Liquid to cover the shank and allow to simmer for 2 hours until flavor has fully developed. Let cool and serve sliced, on country bread with sliced tomato and fresh lettuce. This shank can last one week if covered and refrigerated.

Serve with: *Newton Claret*

Growing up, one of the first things
I learned in my mom's kitchen was how
to make shrimp mousse—it was a basic filling
for dumplings. Years later, when I was study-
ing in Paris, I refined my technique, learning
the secret to creating an airy French-style
mousse. It has just four ingredients, is incredibly tasty, and impressive. I guarantee this
will become a standard in your recipe
repertoire! To save time, you can now
buy frozen shrimp that are already
peeled, cleaned, and deveined.

SHRIMP MOUSSE

Makes 4 cups

1½ *pounds medium shrimp, peeled and deveined*

3 eggs

½ *pound butter, chilled, chopped up into* ⅛*-inch dice*

1 tablespoon truffle oil

Kosher salt and freshly ground white pepper, to taste

In a food processor, place the shrimp and eggs and blend until almost smooth. Add the butter and truffle oil and season. Pulse until butter is incorporated, but still visible in small pieces. Test a small piece for flavor by sautéing or microwaving it. Place in a container, cover, and store in fridge for up to 2 days.

RECOMMENDED BEVERAGES

Celestin Blondeau Pouilly-Fume "Les Robachottes"

Where : Pouilly-Fume, France
Grape: Sauvignon Blanc
Style: Unlike buttery chardonnays, great sauvignons go much better with food. It smells and tastes of apples, pears, and citrus zest, while possessing a stony quality from the Loire Valley's unique soil. Its name comes from the fog or "fume" that covers the vineyards. The relatively high acidity means it can stand up well to acidic foods but also does a wonderful job at cutting through rich, creamy dishes.

Marques de Monistrol Cava

Where : Penedes, Spain
Grape: a blend of Macabeo, Parellada, and sometimes Chardonnay
Style: This sparkling white from Spain is very light, crisp, and acidic, making it a wonderful companion to a variety of shellfish while also providing a wonderful contrast to richer foods. This wine undergoes the same process as champagne but is much cheaper.

When I was younger, I would help my mom spread slices of Pepperidge Farm bread with shrimp mousse and watch her deep fry them. This creates one of the most delicious hors d'oeuvres around and I've included it as a tribute to Mom.

SHRIMP TOAST

Serves 4 to 6

½ pound Shrimp Mousse
1 cup fresh water chestnuts or jicama, cut into ⅛-inch dice
½ cup sliced scallions
1 loaf thinly sliced bread, crusts removed, stale or dried is the best (Take off crust before drying in 200°F oven.)
¼ cup sesame seeds

Prepare a 350°F fryer. In a bowl, gently fold together the mousse, water chestnuts and scallions. Spread a ¼-inch layer of mousse on one side of the bread and sprinkle on sesame seeds. Fry, mousse side down, until golden brown, then flip and continue frying until both sides are brown. Transfer to a paper towel-lined plate, drain well and slice.

Serve with: *Marques de Monistrol Cava*

The set's flowers, direct from Hawaii

STEAMED SHUMAI WITH EDAMAMES AND LEMON BROTH

Serves 4 as a first course

½ pound Shrimp Mousse
¼ cup chopped chervil
½ cup edamames, set aside 12 for garnish
1 quart good chicken stock
Juice of 1 lemon
12 wonton wrappers

Prepare a steamer. In a bowl, gently fold together the mousse, chervil and edamames. To form the shumai, hold 1 wonton wrapper in your hand. Place about 1 tablespoon of the filling in the center of the wrapper. Bring the wrapper up around the filling, pressing it to adhere to the filling and pleating as you go. Continue around the filling. There will be 6 to 8 pleats. Tap the dumpling against the work surface to flatten it. The filling should be level with the top of the dumpling. Repeat with the remaining wrappers and filling. Steam dumplings for about 6 minutes. Meanwhile, heat the broth and when hot, add the lemon juice and season with salt and pepper to taste. Serve 2 to 3 shumai in a shallow pasta bowl with broth. Garnish with edamames.

Serve with: *Celestin Blondeau Pouilly-Fume "Les Rabichottes"*

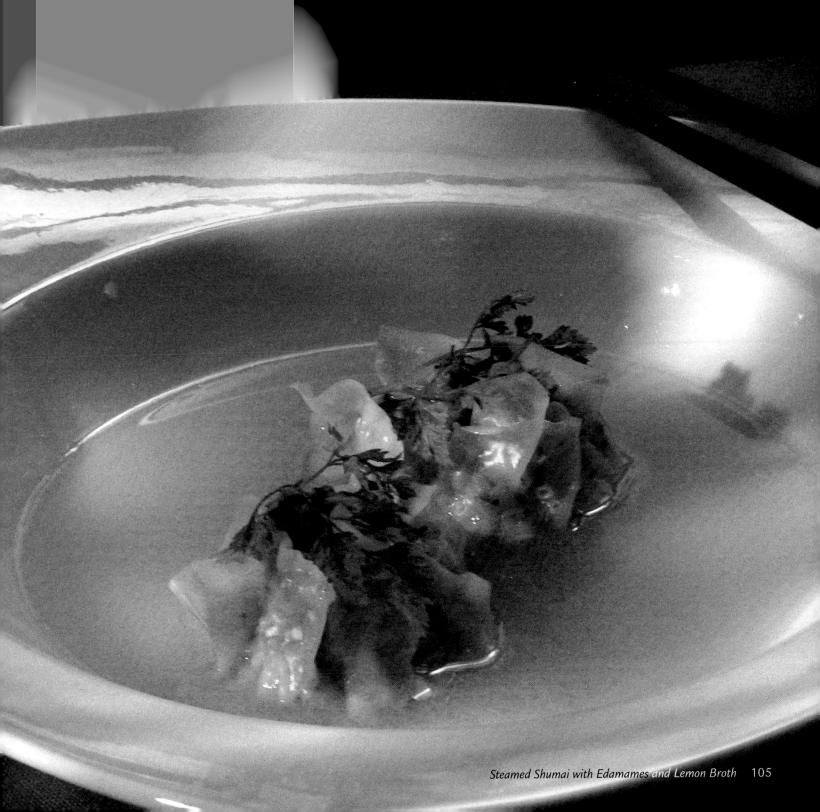

Here I use the Shrimp Mousse as the French often traditionally use it: as a savory crust. This technique produces a wonderful mélange of textures: the firm halibut, creamy mousse, and the crisp crust, achieved by searing the mousse-coated fish. The cool asparagus salad with heat from the sambal and a burst of citrus from the limes, provides further contrast of temperatures and flavors, jazzing up this dish.

SHRIMP-CRUSTED HALIBUT WITH SPICY ASPARAGUS SALAD

Serves 4

4 pieces halibut, 6-ounces each
½ pound Shrimp Mousse
1 pound thin asparagus, ends removed, blanched, shocked, cut into 2-inch spears
1 teaspoon sambal
Juice of 2 limes
1 tablespoon olive oil
Canola or grapeseed oil to cook
Kosher salt and freshly ground black pepper, to taste

Preheat a 400°F oven. Season the dry fillets on both sides and spread a ⅓-inch layer of mousse on one side. In a large non-stick skillet coated lightly with oil, sear the mousse side until lightly brown. Flip and roast in oven for 6 to 8 minutes until done. Meanwhile, in a bowl, toss together the asparagus, sambal, lime juice, and oil. Season with salt and pepper. Place a small mound on a plate and top with halibut.

Serve with: *Celestin Blondeau Pouilly-Fume "Les Rabichottes"*

JACQUES PEPIN'S SHRIMP CUSHION ON WATERCRESS

Serves 4

Who better to create a recipe using Shrimp Mousse than the French chef extraordinaire Jacques Pepin? Just as many terrines do, Jacques encases whole shrimp in a mixture of shrimp mousse and fresh tarragon. He gently cooks each side in butter so that they are golden brown and serves them atop a refreshing watercress salad that has been dressed with red wine vinegar and walnut oil. So simple, so French.

1½ cups Shrimp Mousse
1 tablespoon chopped tarragon
16 shelled shrimp (about ¾ of a pound)
1½ cups fresh bread crumbs
2 tablespoons butter
1 tablespoon olive oil

Mix chopped tarragon with shrimp mousse. Place 4 shrimp tightly together on a plate. Cover with a layer of shrimp mousse. Sprinkle a layer of fresh bread crumbs on top. Turn the "cushion" over, cover the other side with mousse and bread crumbs. Repeat with the rest of the shrimp to make 4 cushions. Melt butter and oil in a large, non-stick pan. Heat and add the cushions. Cook gently for 3 minutes on each side. Serve on the watercress salad.

WATERCRESS SALAD

1 8-ounce bunch of watercress
1 tablespoon red wine vinegar
3 tablespoons walnut oil
Dash of salt and pepper

Mix together at the last moment. Divide salad onto 4 plates with a shrimp cushion on top. Serve immediately.

Serve with: *Marques de Monistrol Cava*

MASTER RECIPE

Growing up, I loved the pungent
salty taste Chinese black beans gave
all sorts of dishes. I've taken their great
flavor and added it to an easy-to-use condiment—Spicy Black Bean Aioli. This versatile
aioli is spiked with garlic, ginger, and fiery
sambal and will add tons of flavor to a
variety of dishes. It's delicious and
dresses up even plain grilled
seafood and chicken — a
dollop goes a long way
to enliven dishes!

SPICY BLACK BEAN AIOLI

Makes 4½ cups

½ cup fermented Chinese black beans
½ cup minced garlic
¼ cup minced ginger
1 bunch scallions sliced, white and green parts separated
½ cup shaoxing wine
¼ cup Dijon mustard
2 tablespoons sambal
4 egg yolks
2½ cups grapeseed or canola oil
Juice of 2 limes
Kosher salt and freshly ground black pepper, to taste

In a wok (preferably non-stick) or sauté pan, coated lightly with oil over high heat, sauté the fermented Chinese black beans, garlic, ginger and scallion whites until soft, about 2 minutes. Deglaze with shaoxing wine and reduce by 90 percent. Transfer to a bowl and let cool. Set up a food processor and add the Dijon mustard, sambal and yolks. Add the cooled fermented Chinese black bean mixture and purée until smooth. Drizzle the oil slowly into the blender to emulsify. Go very slowly with the first ½ cup of oil to get a stiff emulsification. Then you can add the oil a bit faster. Add the lime juice, pulse, and season with kosher salt and freshly ground black pepper to taste. Remove mixture to a bowl and fold in the scallion greens and check again for flavor. Store in a glass jar, covered, in the fridge for up to two weeks.

RECOMMENDED BEVERAGES

Pellegrini Unoaked Chardonnay

Where: Russian River Valley, California
Grape: Chardonnay
Style: A new movement in California to produce chardonnays that have not been matured in oak has produced lighter, crisper, "greener" chardonnays, with more mineral and green apple flavors such as this one.

Livio Felluga Terre Alto

Where: Friuli, Italy
Grape: a blend of 3 grapes—Sauvignon Blanc, Pinot Bianco, Tocai Friulano
Style: This is a crisp, dry white that has a richer body and higher acid making it a wonderful wine to serve with aiolis, vinegars, and oils.

PANKO-CRUSTED COD FISH CAKES

The ultimate cod or crab cake never uses breadcrumbs as a filler, only as a coating. These cakes are 100 percent cod and the Spicy Black Bean Aioli serves as the binder, producing incredibly light, flavorful, and moist cod cakes that are golden and crispy on the outside, coated with Japanese panko flakes.

Serves 4

1½ pounds cod fillet (black cod, butterfish), cut into ½-inch pieces
1 cup Spicy Black Bean Aioli, plus some for garnish
1 cup all-purpose flour
3 eggs, lightly beaten
2 cups panko
Kosher salt and freshly ground black pepper, to taste
1 lime, sliced into 8 wedges

In a large bowl that has been placed within a larger bowl of ice, mix the fish with the Aioli. Using clean hands, make 8 equal patties (mixture will be loose). Dredge in flour, then egg, then panko. In a non-stick sauté pan coated with oil over medium heat, add the cakes and sear until both sides are brown and crispy, about 6 to 8 minutes total. Serve with a small dollop of Aioli and a lime wedge.

Serve with: *Livio Felluga Terre Alto*

Ready to eat!

SKILLET CHICKEN BLT SANDWICH

I love bacon—I consider it the world's perfect meat. While perhaps only Elvis might enjoy my childhood snack of peanut butter and bacon sandwiches, I think everyone will love this one: it combines two things I adore, chicken and bacon, plus crisp lettuce, sweet tomato, and a big dollop of mayo—a necessity for any great BLT. The Aioli gives this sandwich a wonderful salty spicy kick.

Serves 4

8 pieces crisp bacon, cooked in a skillet (reserve the skillet with all the tasty bacon fat)
4 boneless, skinless chicken breasts
1 cup corn starch
½ cup Spicy Black Bean Aioli
1 head iceberg lettuce, shredded
2 ripe tomatoes, sliced
4 buns of choice, preferably toasted
Grapeseed or canola oil for cooking
Kosher salt and freshly ground black pepper, to taste

Reheat the cast iron skillet used for the bacon and top off with oil so there is ¼-inch total fat over medium heat. Season the breasts, dredge in cornstarch, and cook both sides until brown, about 10 minutes total. Meanwhile, toast the buns. Build your sandwich and top with chicken and Aioli.

Serve with: *Pellegrini Unoaked Chardonnay*

I first fished for Mahi-Mahi while shooting a television segment in the Florida Keys—and despite cooking it in every possible way, the tastiest result was the sandwich. The sweet Mahi-Mahi is a great counterpart to the cool, crunchy and spicy slaw.

GRILLED MAHI-MAHI SANDWICH WITH SPICY BLACK BEAN SLAW

Serves 4

4 pieces mahi-mahi, about 6 ounces each
1 tablespoon kucho karo or other chile powder
1 head white cabbage, cored and shredded
1 cup Spicy Black Bean Aioli
2 large dill pickles, cut into ¼-inch dice
4 buns of choice, preferably toasted
Kosher salt and freshly ground black pepper, to taste

Prepare a hot clean grill, wiped or sprayed with canola oil. Season the fish with chile and salt. Place on grill and cook on both sides until cooked through, about 10 minutes total. In a large bowl, mix the cabbage with the Aioli and pickles. Let stand for at least 30 minutes in the fridge before serving. Build a sandwich, topping the fish with the coleslaw.

Serve with: *Pellegrini Unoaked Chardonnay,* but a cold *Corona* would be great too!

Grilled Mahi-Mahi Sandwich with Spicy Black Bean Slaw 117

JASPER WHITE'S CHILLED MUSSELS WITH SPICY BLACK BEAN AIOLI

Makes about 30 hors d'oeuvres

1½ pounds fresh blue mussels, de-bearded and scrubbed
¼ cup shaoxing wine
1 small cucumber
1 cup cabbage, finely chopped
10 sprigs cilantro, chopped, and a few extra for garnish
Sea salt and freshly ground pepper, to taste
1 cup Spicy Black Bean Aioli

My tremendous friend and fellow Boston chef, Jasper White, is THE authority on seafood. He's a chef's chef and he used to have the finest table in town at Jasper's. Now he's having fun frying clams, steaming lobsters, and shucking oysters at his Summer Shacks and he's the envy of us all. These mussels are delicious, super easy, and, when served on ice, make for a dramatic presentation.

Place the mussels and wine in a shallow pot with a tight fitting lid (preferably a straight sided 10- to 12-inch pan) over medium heat and steam the mussels in the wine for 6 to 8 minutes. Do not lift the lid. The mussels should all be open and firm to the touch. Remove the mussels from the pan and allow to cool at room temperature. Reserve the liquid. Remove the mussels from the shell and save one half shell for each mussel. You should have around 30. Keep the shells chilled as well.

Peel the cucumber. Remove the seeds with a spoon. Grate the cucumber on the medium side of a box grater. Toss the grated cucumber with 1 teaspoon of salt and place in a colander or strainer. Allow the cucumber to drain for 15 minutes. Squeeze any excess juice from the cucumber and mix with the cabbage and cilantro. Season with pepper and a bit more salt, if needed. Place about a teaspoon of the mixture in the bottom of the mussel shell, making a little nest for the meat. Place the mussel in the center and keep chilled until ready to serve. Thin the Spicy Black Bean Aioli with about ¼-cup of the reserved liquid from the steamed mussels. Immediately before serving the mussels, use a spoon to nappe each mussel with enough sauce to cover the center. Leave a little of the chopped cucumber mixture showing. Place a tiny leaf of cilantro on each one as a garnish and serve right away. A platter filled with crushed ice will make a very nice presentation.

Serve with: *Livio Felluga Terre Alto*

Sweet and sour is a classic flavor combo in Chinese cuisine and is usually achieved by using vinegar and sugar. At my mom's restaurant she always sweetened it with pineapple, but for this recipe I'm using sweet-tart cranberries for their great flavor and brilliant color. This chutney is so good, you'll find yourself putting it on everything from cheeses, to meat, to poultry!

SWEET AND SOUR CRANBERRY CHUTNEY

Makes 4 cups

> 2 red onions, cut into ½-inch dice
>
> 2 tablespoons minced lemongrass, white part only
>
> 2 cups dried cranberries, such as Craisins, chopped
>
> ½ cup sugar
>
> 2 cups naturally brewed rice vinegar
>
> Grapeseed or canola oil for cooking
>
> Kosher salt and freshly ground black pepper, to taste

In a sauté pan coated lightly with oil over high heat, sauté the onions and lemongrass until soft, about 5 minutes. Season with kosher salt and freshly ground black pepper and check for flavor. Add cranberries and sugar and deglaze with naturally brewed rice vinegar. Reduce by 75 percent, or until liquid is absorbed. Check again for seasoning. When cool, transfer to a container, cover, and store in fridge for up to two weeks.

RECOMMENDED BEVERAGES

Newton Unfiltered Pinot Noir

Where: Sonoma, California
Grape: Pinot Noir
Style: Due to the fact that this is unfiltered and unfined, this is a big bodied wine with very robust flavors of black cherry, raspberry, earth, and a touch of smoke. The dark fruit flavors enrich the nuances of cranberries, enhancing all dishes made with the Sweet and Sour Cranberry Chutney. A great wine to pair with gamey meats like duck due to strong fruit overtones.

Newton Unfiltered Chardonnay

Where: Sonoma, California
Grape: Chardonnay
Style: There are some whites designed to complement richer dishes. Napa and Carneros chardonnays, with their characteristic creaminess and burnt oakiness, can hold their own with very powerful flavor combinations.

Duck and fruit are a classic French pairing: the sweet fruit complements the rich gamey meat while the peppercorns are also a natural match with beef and duck, their spiciness balancing the richness and sweetness of this dish. The potato discs are très français—cooking them in duck fat is the most decadent and delicious way to eat potatoes in my opinion!

PEPPERCORN DUCK BREAST WITH SWEET AND SOUR CRANBERRY CHUTNEY AND POTATO DISCS

Serves 4

4 duck breasts, fat trimmed, skin side scored
½ cup coarse ground peppercorns (preferably black, green and pink mixed in equal quantities, but just black would work fine)
2 large Yukon gold potatoes, baked skin on until al dente, about 45 minutes at 350°F
Grapeseed or canola oil for cooking
Kosher salt, to taste
¾ cup Sweet and Sour Cranberry Chutney

Season the duck breasts on both sides with salt and the peppercorn mix. Peel the potato and slice into ½-inch discs, and season with kosher salt and freshly ground black pepper. In a sauté pan over low-medium heat, place the breasts skin side down. Let them render (melt fat away) until the skin is brown and crispy, about 10 minutes. Transfer to a plate, meat side down and let rest. In the same pan, with the luscious duck fat, turn the pan on high. Add the potato slices and brown on both sides, about 3 to 5 minutes a side. Transfer to a plate lined with paper towels. Add back the breasts, this time meat side down, and sear for 3 to 5 minutes for medium rare. Flip onto skin side just to re-crisp and transfer to a cutting board and let rest. Lay out slices of the potato on a plate, slice the duck and lay on top. Top with Sweet and Sour Cranberry Chutney.

Serve with: *Newton Pinot Noir*

I LOVE sweet and sour pork fried rice and grew up eating dishes and dishes of it. Now that I'm a New Englander, I've added a New England twist in the form of Sweet and Sour Cranberry Chutney to this Chinese classic with very tasty results.

SWEET AND SOUR PORK FRIED RICE

Serves 4

3 eggs, beaten
1 pound ground pork
1 bunch scallions sliced, white and green parts separated
6 cups cooked long grain rice, preferably day old so it's nice and dry (In a rush, place cooked rice on a sheet tray and place in freezer to cool and dry.)
1 cup Sweet and Sour Cranberry Chutney, plus 2 tablespoons for garnish
1 tablespoon naturally brewed soy sauce
Grapeseed or canola oil for cooking
Kosher salt and freshly ground black pepper, to taste

In a wok (preferably non-stick) or sauté pan coated well with oil over high heat, add eggs (they should puff up immediately), stir quickly and transfer to a plate lined with paper towels. Place the wok back over high heat and add the pork. Break up and cook until browned, then add the scallion whites and mix. Add the rice, Chutney, naturally brewed soy sauce, and the eggs. Season with kosher salt and freshly ground black pepper and check for flavor. Serve in a large bowl and garnish with scallion greens and additional Chutney.

Serve with: *Newton Unfiltered Chardonnay*

Crab rangoons, a popular Chinese-American appetizer, are usually composed of crabmeat and cream cheese. I am a huge fan of cranberry cheesecake—the tartness of the berries balances the richness of the cream cheese perfectly. I thought the addition of cranberries, via this Chutney, would be equally delicious in these dumplings. I love this updated version and think you will too.

CRANBERRY-CRAB RANGOON

Makes 10 to 12 rangoons

1 pound picked, fresh crab meat, (snow, blue)
¼ pound cream cheese, softened
1 cup Sweet and Sour Cranberry Chutney, plus some for garnish
3 tablespoons chopped chives, save 1 tablespoon for garnish
1 package thin square wonton skins, defrosted
1 egg mixed with 2 tablespoons water
Grapeseed or canola oil for cooking
Kosher salt and freshly ground black pepper, to taste

In a large bowl, mix the crab, cream cheese, chutney, and chives. Season with kosher salt and freshly ground black pepper and check for flavor. Lay out 4 to 6 skins, lightly brush the edges with egg wash and place a small mound of the mix in the middle. Top with second skin and press firmly to seal. This is very important so the rangoons do not burst and leak. Repeat until the filling is gone. Preheat a large sauté pan coated with ¼-inch of oil over medium-high heat. Add as many rangoons as the pan can hold in one layer. Shallow fry until golden brown, flip and fry other side until golden brown. Transfer rangoons to a plate lined with paper towels. Place a small mound of chutney on a plate, surround with 3 rangoons, garnish with chives and serve hot.

Serve with: *Newton Unfiltered Chardonnay*

MELISSA KELLY'S CRISP MAINE LOBSTER-POTATO CAKE WITH ORANGE SAUCE AND SWEET AND SOUR CRANBERRY VINAIGRETTE

For this master Sweet and Sour Cranberry Chutney, I invited renowned New England chef Melissa Kelly to the show. She used another New England star—Maine Lobster—and created an awesome and gorgeous dish.

Serves 4

4 Yukon gold potatoes, boiled, skins on
1 bunch scallions, thinly sliced
5 tablespoons extra virgin olive oil
2 sprigs tarragon
2 1½-pound lobsters (cooked, shelled and meat cut into 1-inch dice)
Juice of 2 oranges, julienne zest and reserve
3 tablespoons unsalted butter
⅓ cup Sweet and Sour Cranberry Chutney
1 to 2 tablespoons water
1 cup frisee
1 bunch chives
2 sprigs Italian parsley
Kosher salt and freshly ground black pepper, to taste

Place warm potatoes in a bowl, crush with scallions and 3 tablespoons extra virgin olive oil and season with salt and pepper. Mix in lobster meat and chopped tarragon, and spoon into ring molds. Place in refrigerator and chill. Pour orange juice into a saucepan over high heat. Once it begins to simmer, whisk in butter, season with salt and white pepper and keep warm. In a small bowl, mix chutney with 1 tablespoon oil, thin with water and reserve. In a separate bowl, mix greens with herb leaves and orange zest. Set aside. Heat a skillet over high heat and add remaining 1 tablespoon oil to pan. Brown potato cakes on both sides. While the lobster-potato cakes are browning, dress your salad. To serve, place lobster-potato cake in the center of the plate, ladle a small amount of the orange sauce around, top with the salad, and remove the ring.

Serve with: *Newton Unfiltered Chardonnay*

*This paste is the secret to all
the spicy dishes from the Szechwan
province of China, their famous heat coming
from a tiny little nugget called the Szechwan
peppercorn. Its rich spicy flavor is great
with everything: from meat, to
poultry, to seafood.*

SZECHWAN PEPPERCORN PASTE

Makes 3 cups

  1 cup Szechwan peppercorns
  2 cups grapeseed oil
  ¼ cup white peppercorns, toasted until lightly smoking
  2 large yellow onions, sliced
  2 tablespoons minced ginger
  ½ cup honey
  Grapeseed or canola oil to cook
  Kosher salt, to taste

Place peppercorns in a dry pan (preferably a cast iron skillet) and toast until smoking over medium heat. Add the oil and heat over low flame for 30 minutes. Let cook and strain and discard seeds. In a spice grinder, grind the white peppercorns until fine. In a wok coated lightly with oil, sauté the onions and ginger until soft. Add shaoxing wine and reduce by 95 percent. Season with salt to taste. Transfer to a food processor, add the white peppercorns and honey, and purée until smooth, drizzling in the infused oil to form an emulsion. When cool, transfer to a container, cover, and store in the fridge for up to two weeks.

RECOMMENDED BEVERAGES

Newton Chardonnay

Where: Sonoma, California
Grape: Chardonnay
Style: Because this wine is unfiltered and unfined, it possesses more subtle, earthier nuances. It is a "big" white that is still medium-bodied enough to enhance light seafood dishes like shrimp and conch. The rich flavor nicely balances spicy heat making it a great match for dishes using this master.

Bourgueils Cabernet Franc

Where : Loire Valley, France
Grape: Cabernet Franc
Style: This grape is the parent of cabernet sauvignon and is not as full bodied but is more fragrant. The wine features richer fruit notes, blackberry and red currants are presented in a lighter and much less tannic bodied wine, allowing the wine to blend with a wider spectrum of food.

This came from the memory of a delicious dish I had some time ago: steamed asparagus was flash fried with Szechwan peppercorn oil and served with beef. I've added noodles for a tasty stir fry dish that is a one dish meal as well.

SZECHWAN BEEF AND ASPARAGUS NOODLES

Serves 4

1½ pounds flank steak, sliced ¼-inch thin, against the grain, on the bias
1 pound thin asparagus, ends cut off, blanched until just crisp in salted water,
   shocked in ice water
½ cup Szechwan Peppercorn Paste
½ pound rotini, blanched
Grapeseed or canola oil to cook
Kosher salt, to taste

In a wok or sauté pan coated lightly with oil over medium-high heat, stir fry the beef for 4 minutes. Add the asparagus, Paste and noodles and stir fry until heated thoroughly, about 4 minutes. Check for flavor.

Serve with: *Bourgueils Cabernet Franc*

Ming really appreciating the camera crew after realizing how heavy the 'steady-cam' was.

CRISPY FARM RAISED CONCH WITH LEMON-SZECHWAN DIPPING SAUCE

I love conch and eat tons of it whenever I'm in the islands. Luckily it's becoming more available up north—we even carry it at Blue Ginger now, getting it from the Caicos Conch Farm in Turks & Caicos where farm-raising is producing excellent quality conch. Like calamari, it can be a challenge to properly cook: either fry it quickly, cook it slowly over lower heat, or serve it ceviche-style. Here, I briefly marinate the conch in fresh lemon juice and cilantro, coat it with a mixture of cornstarch, rice flour, and sugar and deep fry it. Adding lemon to the paste makes a wonderfully acidic but spicy dipping sauce that is utterly addictive with these fried morsels.

Serves 4

Juice of 3 lemons
¼ cup chopped cilantro
2 pounds conch, cleaned and sliced thinly
1 cup cornstarch
1 cup rice flour
¼ cup powdered sugar
¼ cup Szechwan Peppercorn Paste
Canola oil for frying
Kosher salt for seasoning

Preheat a heavy bottom stock pot or use a fryer set at 375°F filled with oil. In a bowl, mix together the lemon juice and cilantro and marinate the conch for 1 minute only. In another bowl, mix the cornstarch, rice flour, and sugar together and transfer the drained conch to the flour mixture. Using a spider or strainer, shake off excess flour and place in the fryer or stock pot. Fry until GB&D (golden brown and delicious), only 2 minutes maximum, and transfer to a plate lined with paper towels. Lightly season with salt. Meanwhile, in a non-reactive sauce pan, heat the lemon juice and cilantro mixture until boiling, then whisk in the Paste. Check for seasoning and serve in a small ramekin with the hot conch.

Serve with: *Newton Unfiltered Chardonnay*

Crispy Farm Raised Conch with Lemon-Szechwan Dipping Sauce 135

I love squab, also known as the "royal bird". It has much more flavor than chicken and it's fun serving everyone an individual bird. Because of its gamier meat, it can stand up to the spicy Szechwan Peppercorn Paste wonderfully. In place of a more traditional bread stuffing is the addictive garlic chive sticky rice.

OVEN ROASTED SZECHWAN SQUAB STUFFED WITH GARLIC CHIVE STICKY RICE

Serves 4

4 whole squab, eviscerated, rubbed with Szechwan Peppercorn Paste inside
    and out and lightly salted
3 cups cooked Koshi Hikari
1 cup chopped garlic chives
1 tablespoon soy sauce
Kosher salt, to taste

Preheat oven to 500°F. In a bowl, mix together the rice and chives and add soy sauce. Stuff the squab with the rice, place in a large roasting pan or on a baking sheet and roast until skin is brown, about 10 to 15 minutes. Turn oven down to 250°F, tent with foil if necessary, and roast for an additional 10 minutes. Transfer to a cutting board and let rest for 5 minutes before carving into pieces. Serve over rice.

Serve with: *Bourgueils Cabernet Franc*

MOM AND POP'S MA LA SAUCE AND COLD NOODLE SALAD

Serves 4

½ pound fresh noodles, boiled and chilled
1 cup chicken, cooked and shredded
½ cup hot house cucumber, cut into thin strips
½ cup red pepper, cut into thin strips (pepper can be skinned to improve texture)
2 scallions, cut into 1-inch long thin strips, both white and green parts
½ to 1 cup Szechwan Peppercorn Paste (Ma La Sauce)
Kosher salt and freshly ground black pepper, to taste

Place all vegetables and Ma La sauce (to taste) in a large bowl with noodles and mix well, preferably by hand. Season to taste.

Serve with: *Newton Unfiltered Chardonnay*

In Chinese, "ma" means to be numb while "la" means spicy—so "ma la" is a numbing spiciness which is what Szechwan peppercorns do! The Chinese love noodles and this cold noodle salad features cooling cucumber, sweet red peppers, and chicken, flavored with the spicy Szechwan Peppercorn Paste.

Ming practices introduction.

MASTER RECIPE

At Blue Ginger, we make
gigantic vats of this sauce —it's been on
the menu since day one and there would
probably be a rebellion if we took it off! This
sauce is awesome with everything and
is just what a dipping sauce should
be: a little salty, a little tart,
and a little spicy.

THREE CHILE DIPPING SAUCE

Makes 4 cups

4 red or green jalapeños (or 2 red, 2 green), stemmed, minced with seeds

6 serrano chiles, stemmed, minced with seeds

8 Thai bird chiles (dried are fine if you can't find fresh)

1 bunch scallions, ¼-inch chopped

1 cup rice vinegar

3 cups soy sauce

In a bowl, mix all ingredients together. Store in the fridge for up to two weeks. Mix well before using as the chiles will settle.

Leon Beyer Gewürztraminer

Where: Alsace, France
Grape: Gewürztraminer
Style: Gewürztraminer means "spicy grape" and this wine has the aroma of lychees and spices with a sweet edge and very rich mouth. Its cooling sweetness is an ideal match for spicier dishes.

Sapporo Japanese Beer

Where: Sapporo, Japan
Style: This crisp lager is fantastic with 'finger food' and sauces with kick making in a great accompaniment to dishes served with the Three Chile Dipping Sauce. Lagers are always good choices with food since they aren't heavy, fruity, or malty, changing the flavors of the dish. This particular brand is sold in 22-ounce cans that are designed to be shared with friends like bottles of wine—a common practice in Japan.

3 MUSHROOM LUMPIAS AND HEALTHIER MUSHROOM WRAPS

Lumpias are the popular Philippine version of Chinese egg rolls. I grew up filling egg rolls with mushrooms and in this version I use three kinds for varied texture and taste, but you can easily use just one type of mushroom if you prefer. For a healthier alternative and to avoid deep frying, place the filling in red leaf lettuce, roll, and serve with the dipping sauce.

Makes 12 lumpias or wraps

2 tablespoons minced garlic
1 tablespoon minced ginger
2 red sliced onions
1 pound shiitake mushrooms, stemmed, cut into ¼-inch slices
1 pound oyster mushrooms, hand ripped into halves or quarters, lengthwise
1 pound maitake mushrooms, 'florets' taken off with a knife, stem trimmed and julienned
2 cups dry white wine
1 package lumpia wrappers
2 eggs mixed with ¼ cup water
1 head red leaf lettuce, washed, spun dry
1 bunch mint, washed, spun dry
Grapeseed or canola oil for frying
Kosher salt and freshly ground black pepper, to taste
½ cup Three Chile Dipping Sauce for serving

In a wok coated with oil over medium heat, sauté the garlic, ginger, onions until soft, about 1 minute. Add the shiitakes, sauté 2 minutes, then add the oysters and maitakes. Season with salt and freshly ground black pepper to taste. Deglaze with white wine and completely reduce. Check for flavor. For the wraps, place small mound of hot mushrooms on lettuce and roll free form. Serve with dipping sauce. Transfer to a tray and let cool to room temperature. Place in fridge or in the freezer to speed up cooling process.

To make the lumpias, lay out 5 sheets of lumpia wrappers on a work surface with a corner near you. Place small mound of the filling a little above the corner and bring the near corner of the wrapper over the filling to enclose it. Brush the edges with egg wash, roll tightly toward the middle of the wrapper, then fold in the sides and continue to roll to make a sticklike spring roll ¼- to ½-inch in diameter. Make the roll as thin as possible. Rest the roll seam side down for 2 minutes and repeat with the remaining wrappers and filling.

Heat a fryer or stock pot with oil to 350°F. Add lumpias and fry until GB&D (golden brown & delicious). Remove with a large mesh spoon and drain on paper towels. Repeat with remaining lumpias. Slice on the bias and serve on a bed of lettuce garnished with mint leaves and ramekins of dipping sauce.

Serve with: *Sapporo* or, equally tasty, *Michelob Ultra*

There aren't many people that can resist fried food and tempura is an addictive way to eat your veggies! When I was training in Osaka I learned the classic technique for preparing tempura and over the years, through trial and error, I've created what I think is the best tempura batter recipe, using club soda and eliminating eggs for a lighter coating and adding a small amount of chile powder for a bit of a kick. But I'll let you be the judge.

VEGETARIAN TEMPURA

Serves 4

2 cups rice flour
1 tablespoon kucho karu chile powder
1 quart cold club soda
1 large sweet potato, peeled, sliced ¼-inch lengthwise
1 daikon, peeled and sliced into long batons (3-inches x ¼-inch x ¼-inch)
1 Japanese eggplant, sliced ¼-inch long bias slices
1 bunch scallions, ends trimmed off
Grapeseed or canola oil for frying
Kosher salt and freshly ground black pepper, to taste
½ cup Three Chile Dipping Sauce

In a large bowl, add flour and chile powder and whisk in the soda until a pancake batter consistency is achieved. Fill a fryer or stockpot ⅓-full with oil and heat to 350°F. Dip the vegetables in the batter, shake off excess, and fry until GB&D (golden brown & delicious). Drain on paper towels and season lightly with salt while still hot. Serve with dipping sauce.

Serve with: *Sapporo*

This dish is influenced by one of my most favorite places in the world, Hawaii. Sweet jumbo shrimp are skewered with pineapple and marinated in the Three Chile Dipping Sauce before being grilled. The pineapple caramelizes on the grill and this dish is the ultimate in salty, sweet, and spicy.

GRILLED SATAYS OF MARINATED JUMBO SHRIMP AND PINEAPPLE

Serves 4

12 jumbo shrimp, peeled, deveined, butterflied, tail on
1 medium pineapple, peeled and cut into 3-inch spears
1 cup Three Chile Dipping Sauce
Grapeseed or canola oil to cook
Kosher salt, to taste

Prepare a grill, cleaned and wiped or sprayed with canola oil. To make the satays, wrap a shrimp around a piece of pineapple and thread 2 parallel skewers through to hold the shrimp and the pineapple in place. Marinate for 10 minutes in the Three Chile Dipping Sauce, then grill until done, about 6 to 8 minutes total. Serve with additional dipping sauce.

Serve with: *Leon Beyer Gewürztraminer*

KEN ORINGER'S STEAMED BLACK BASS WITH HOT GARLIC OIL, THREE CHILE DIPPING SAUCE, AND CANDIED ORANGE

Ken is not only a fantastic friend but a truly amazing chef at both of his Boston restaurants Clio and Uni, garnering many awards over the years. In true Ken fashion, he has taken the master and created a dish that features a complex layering of flavors and an elegant presentation. Black bass is steamed with citrus zest, kaffir lime and black beans and served with hot garlic oil, Three Chile Dipping Sauce, and candied orange, creating an explosion of tastes that complement each other in a very unique dish.

Serves 4

4 black bass fillets
3 tablespoons butter (softened)
1 tablespoon lemon zest, chopped
1 tablespoon orange zest, chopped
1 tablespoon lime zest, chopped
3 tablespoons kaffir lime leaf, shredded
¼ cup garlic oil
2 tablespoons Chinese black beans, chopped
⅓ cup candied orange peel (recipe follows)
2 tablespoons Korean pepper threads
2 bunches cilantro
Kosher salt and freshly ground black pepper, to taste

Preheat oven to 400°F and set up a bamboo steamer to accommodate all fish. Season fillets with salt and pepper, rub with softened butter, and place on a plate. Scatter citrus zests, kaffir leaf and black beans on top of the fish and set aside. When ready to steam, put fish plate into steamer (skin side up) and place steamer in the bottom of the oven. Let steam until just cooked, about 8 minutes.

Meanwhile, heat garlic oil until boiling. When fish is done, place on serving tray and mix the cooking juices with the Three Chile Dipping Sauce and pour over the fish. Top with the hot garlic oil, Korean pepper treads, cilantro and candied orange peel and serve.

Serve with: *Leon Beyer Gewürztraminer*

CANDIED ORANGE PEEL

1 orange, rind only
1 cup sugar
Water

Peel sections of rind using a vegetable peeler and make sure there is no white pith. Place cold water in a saucepan, add the orange rind, and bring to boil. Strain and repeat this process five times.

Add 1 cup of water and 1 cup of sugar to the blanched rind in the saucepan and cook on low heat until translucent. Place candied orange rind on a parchment-lined sheet pan and allow to dry in a 200°F oven for several hours until crisp. Reserve.

Ken Orringer's Steamed Black Bass with Hot Garlic Oil, Three Chile Dipping Sauce, and Candied Orange

MASTER RECIPE

People usually opt for chicken or beef stock over the bland vegetable stock when cooking but now that cooks are increasingly health-conscious, more are reaching for vegetable stock in its place. The age-old challenge is to keep something "healthy" but also brimming with flavor. After many tries, I've figured it out with the addition of a secret ingredient: dried shiitakes. These mushrooms mimic the depth that meat and bones usually give to stock. The addition of the sweet potato gives a velvety viscosity due to its starch. Now you have a richly-flavored stock which can be the basis for so many awesome meals that will please your "veghead" and "non-vegheads" alike.

VEGETARIAN BROTH

Makes 4 quarts

4 large carrots, washed and roughly chopped

4 yellow onions, peeled and roughly chopped

1 bunch celery, washed and roughly chopped

3 heads fennel, roughly chopped

1 small hand ginger, washed and sliced

1 large sweet potato, peeled and sliced

4 stalks lemongrass, stemmed and pounded

2 apples, washed and split

2 bay leaves

2 heads garlic, split

4 sprigs of thyme

½ pound dried whole shiitake mushrooms, rinsed

1 tablespoon black peppercorns, toasted

2 tablespoons soy sauce

Grapeseed oil for cooking

In a large stock pot coated very lightly with oil over medium-high heat, sauté the carrots, onions, celery, fennel, ginger, sweet potato, and lemongrass. Sauté until caramelized, about 10 minutes. Add apples, bay leaves, garlic, thyme, shiitakes, peppercorns, and soy sauce. Cover with cold water (at least 4 quarts). Bring to a simmer and cook for 1½ hours until the broth has reduced by 20 percent. Taste for seasoning. Strain and store in fridge for up to 2 weeks or freeze for 2 months.

RECOMMENDED BEVERAGES

St. Michael Eppan Pinot Blanc

Where: South Tyrol, Italy
Grape: Pinot Blanc
Style: This wine is filled with Bartlett pear and citrus aromas, very crisp, and elegant, with a soft finish. Pinot Blanc is gaining ground in the world market as a crisper and less sweet alternative to pinot gris/grigio.

Avila Pinot Noir

Where: San Luis Obispo County, California
Grape: Pinot Noir
Style: Because of the finicky nature of this grape, quality versions of the wine never come inexpensively. This makes the quality of this wine all the more special. It features complex aromas of boiled raspberry, cherry, mixed spice and vanilla. It is soft and round on the palate and has a slightly sweet finish.

THREE ONION SOUP

Serves 6 to 8

While not that common in France, you will find onion soup at any bistro catering to tourists including the famous Au Pied du Cochon in the Les Halles area of Paris. It is open all night—a reminder of the fact that Les Halles used to be abuzz 24 hours a day due to the market activity. All purveyors assembled in this neighborhood to sell their produce, fish, game, and dairy and this area was quite literally the belly of Paris! When my mother was pregnant and in Paris, she craved onion soup and became a regular at Au Pied du Cochon. Here's my version which features not one, but three types of onions, as well as shiitakes. However, I follow tradition and finish it gratineed in an oven crock. Some things you just shouldn't change!

4 yellow onions, peeled, sliced
5 shallots, sliced
2 bunch scallions, trimmed into 1-inch pieces
6 cloves garlic, thinly sliced
1 pound large fresh shiitakes, stemmed and ¼-inch sliced
1 bottle red wine
2 tablespoons soy sauce
1 tablespoon minced thyme
1½ quarts Vegetarian Broth
Extra virgin olive oil for cooking
Kosher salt and freshly ground peppercorn, to taste
1 crusty baguette, sliced in 1-inch thick pieces, and toasted dry
1 cup shredded gruyere cheese
4 oven proof crock pots

Preheat the broiler. In a large stock pot coated with extra virgin olive oil over medium-high heat, add the onions, shallots, scallions, and garlic. Season well, and sauté until browned, about 20 minutes. Deglaze with wine and reduce by 90 percent. Add soy sauce, thyme, and Broth and bring to a simmer. Check for flavor and reduce by 25 percent. Transfer the soup into the crock pots and top with toasted baguette. Cover with cheese and broil until brown and bubbly. Enjoy, and be careful, it'll be really hot.

Serve with: *Avila Pinot Noir*

Three Onion Soup   153

Many consider risotto the ultimate comfort food that just happens to sport an urbane name. Instead of using the traditional Arborio rice, I use a sushi rice called Koshi Hikari. This is the Cadillac of sushi rices and makes phenomenal risotto due to the fact that it has a 30 percent absorption rate as opposed to 20 percent for Arborio (and only 10 percent for long grain). The grains absorb the flavor of the rich stock, garlic, and shallots while the dish receives added taste, texture, and dimension from fresh spinach and shiitake mushrooms. The juice of one lime before serving brightens the dish and the tart citrus complements the creaminess.

SHIITAKE-SPINACH RISOTTO

Serves 4

4 shallots, cut into very small dice
1 tablespoon garlic, chopped
2 cups shiitake caps, cut into ¼-inch slices
2 cups Koshi Hikari
3 to 4 cups hot Vegetarian Broth
2 cups finely shredded spinach (washed, spun dry before slicing), save ½ cup for garnish
Juice of 1 lime
Grapeseed oil for cooking
Kosher salt and freshly ground black pepper, to taste

Heat a medium saucepan over medium heat. Add the grapeseed oil and swirl to coat the pan. When the oil shimmers add the shallots, garlic, mushrooms, and rice. Sauté, stirring, about 3 minutes. Add a ladleful of the stock and continue to cook, stirring, until the liquid is absorbed. Add more stock and continue to cook and stir, allowing each addition of stock to be absorbed before adding the next, until the rice is cooked through and has a creamy consistency, but the grains are still individual. Season with the salt and pepper to taste and toss with 1½ cups of spinach. Meanwhile, toss the remaining ½-cup of spinach with juice, a touch of oil and season. Place the risotto in soup plates and top with a little spinach salad.

Serve with: *Avila Pinot Noir*

Instool of the traditional Coq au Vin, here is Legumes aux Vin. Braising a selection of vegetables in red wine and vegetable stock produces a richly flavored dish—serve with hot brown rice and you can enjoy la cuisine française with zero guilt!

LÉGUMES AUX VIN

Serves 4

2 red onions, cut into 1-inch dice
1 tablespoon minced ginger
1 pound carrot nubs
4 ribs of celery, cut into 1-inch pieces
2 sweet potatoes, peeled, squared off, cut into 1-inch dice
½ pound white button mushrooms, prepped, large ones cut in half
2 cups whole Napoli tomatoes, drained
1 bottle red wine
1½ quarts Vegetarian Broth
Grapeseed oil for cooking
Kosher salt and freshly ground black pepper, to taste
Serve with hot brown rice

In a large stock pot coated very lightly with oil over medium heat, sauté the onions, ginger, carrots, celery, potatoes, and mushrooms. Season with kosher salt and freshly ground pepper to taste. Add tomatoes and deglaze with red wine. Reduce by 50 percent, then add stock. Bring to a simmer and cook until potatoes are cooked through, about 45 minutes. Check again for seasoning and serve in large bowls over rice.

Serve with: *Avila Pinot Noir*

JACQUES PEPIN'S RED SNAPPER À LA NAGE

Serves 4

Presenting red snapper in a classically French fashion, master chef Jacques Pepin creates an elegant dish of red snapper with the delicate flavors of white wine, julienned leeks, mushrooms, and the master Vegetarian Broth. A nage is an aromatic broth cooking liquid that is reduced and, quite frequently, finished with butter ("monté au beurre").

4 red snapper fillets (about 5 ounces each), boneless with skin on
1 cucumber, peeled, seeded, and cut into 2- by 1-inch slices
1½ cups mushrooms, julienned
1 cup leeks, julienned
½ cup dry white wine
1 cup Vegetarian Broth
½ teaspoon salt and pepper
4 tablespoons butter
¼ cup black olives, cut in ½-inch dice

Blanch the cucumber in salted water for 1 minute. Drain and sauté in butter, seasoning with salt and pepper. Set aside. Place the stock, wine, mushrooms and leeks in a saucepan and bring to a boil. Boil for 2 minutes. Add fish and bring back to a boil; lower heat and simmer gently for 2 minutes. Transfer fish to a platter. Reduce stock over high heat for 2 minutes, whisk in butter, and bring to a strong boil. Pour over fish, sprinkle with olives and garnish with cucumber.

Serve with: *St. Michael Eppan Pinot Blanc*

MASTER RECIPE

Many that come to Blue Ginger say that one
of their favorite things isn't even on the menu—it's
in the bread basket. My pastry chef Marina Brancely
bakes 30 loaves of brioche each day! Our brioche are
buttery loaves with a soft, crumbly texture due to
the addition of cornmeal. We also use this
brioche for sweet and savory pastries
but sliced and toasted with a
schmear of butter is simply
unbelievable too.

CLASSIC BRIOCHE WITH CORNMEAL

Makes 3 loaves

| 2 ounces milk, 70°F (room temperature)
| ¾ ounce (1½ cakes) yeast
| 4 cups bread flour
| ¾ cup cornmeal
| ¼ cup sugar
| 1½ teaspoons salt
| 14 ounces (approximately 7 extra large) eggs
| 3 sticks sweet butter, softened

In a small bowl, combine the milk and the yeast, set aside. In the bottom of a 5-quart Kitchen Aid mixing bowl, combine the flour and cornmeal. Make a well, add yeast/milk mixture, and make a very loose paste using some of the flour inside the well. Cover lightly with some of the flour and let this sponge sit until it breaks through the dusting of flour.

Add the eggs, sugar, and salt and mix with a paddle until the gluten starts to develop. Add the softened butter in small pieces and continue mixing on speed 2 until gluten is fully developed, approximately 20 to 30 minutes. Place in a plastic container, cover with plastic wrap and bulk ferment in the refrigerator overnight.

At this point the dough may be shaped and proofed or frozen for 3 to 4 weeks. To freeze, divide into 3 equal portions, wrap well in plastic, and place in freezer. To thaw, place in refrigerator for 8 hours or overnight. Then shape, proof, and bake according to directions.

To bake immediately: Place shaped loaves into well-greased loaf pans and allow to rise until they have increased 1½ times in size (approximately 1½ hours at 80°F).

Brush with egg wash and bake at 300°F for approximately 30 to 40 minutes.

RECOMMENDED BEVERAGES

Cloudy Bay Chardonnay

Where: Marlborough, New Zealand
Grape: Chardonnay
Style: This chardonnay has vibrant flavors and flinty tones and is a refreshing contrast to heavier foods such as braised chicken, bread stuffings, and the brioche wrapped salmon.

Cinnamon Coffee

Add ½ teaspoon of ground cinnamon to your best coffee and brew according to directions. Try blending your coffee at the market to create your own unique flavor. Here at Blue Ginger, we have a custom blend of Millstone beans—Aztec, French Roast, and Guatemalan.

Café au Lait

Brew a pot of double-strength coffee and pour coffee into mugs with equal parts steamed milk. If serving in the evening, a shot of Kahlua is a nice addition.

To our Classic Brioche we often add sweet caramelized onions and fiery sambal in the form of a tasty condiment so good you could happily eat it alone. This tender buttery bread benefits from the sweet-spicy compote which lends a sweet subtle flavor. This bread is brilliant alone but makes sandwiches that are over-the-top good.

SAVORY CARAMELIZED ONION AND SAMBAL BRIOCHE

Makes 3 loaves

1 recipe Classic Brioche
1 recipe Caramelized Onion Sambal Compote (below)
2 eggs, beaten

CARAMELIZED ONION SAMBAL COMPOTE

¼ cup olive oil
2½ pounds (approximately 5 medium) onions, sliced
½ cup honey
¼ cup sambal

Heat olive oil in a large sauté pan and add the onions, cooking until caramelized. Turn off heat and add the honey and sambal, stirring to combine and allow to cool completely. Add compote to one recipe of brioche dough and mix until fully incorporated. The following day, after dough has been allowed to bulk ferment overnight, remove from refrigerator, and divide dough into three equal loaves. Put into well-greased loaf pans and allow to rise until it has increased 1½ times in size (approximately 1½ hours at 80°F).

Brush with egg wash and bake at 300°F for approximately 30 to 40 minutes.

Serve with: Believe it or not, *whipped butter*—it's always better with butter!

It's hard to find a lousy coffee cake—even the bad ones are usually kind of good. Here, the buttery brioche provides a rich base that is covered with a perfect streusel filling that includes spices, butter, brown sugar, and oats. It's rolled jelly-roll style and baked. The result is quite beyond mediocre, yielding buttery slices that are laced with streusel and fragrant with five spice, cinnamon, and ginger.

SWEET FIVE SPICED COFFEE CAKE

Makes 3 loaves

1 recipe Classic Brioche
1 recipe Five Spiced Streusel Filling (below)
2 eggs, beaten

Serve with: *Cinnamon Coffee*

FIVE SPICED STREUSEL FILLING*

6 ounces oats, old-fashioned
9 ounces butter, cold, cubed
6 ounces bread flour
6 ounces dark brown sugar
6 ounces sugar
2 tablespoons five spice powder
2 tablespoons cinnamon, ground
2 tablespoons ginger, ground

Make Brioche recipe the day before and have ready. Make the streusel filling by combining the dry ingredients with a paddle attachment in a stand mixer, then cutting in cold butter and mixing until crumbly (be careful not to over-mix!).

Divide the dough into three equal loaves. Flatten the rectangle so it's about 1-inch thick, cover with a layer of streusel topping, and roll up like a jelly roll. Place loaves, seam side down, into well-greased loaf pans and allow to rise until they are 1½ times in size. Brush with egg wash and bake at 300°F for approximately 30 to 40 minutes.

Streusel may be stored in refrigerator or freezer until ready to use for up to 2 weeks.

SALMON EN CROUTE

Brioche dough is a lot more versatile than people think. In addition to bread and pastries, it is amazing when it envelops meat and fish in the French style "en croute", an item which is very popular at the stylish traiteurs, or gourmet take-away shops like Fauchon in Paris. Here a whole salmon fillet is brushed with the Spicy-Sweet Caramelized Onion Sambal Compote, wrapped in the brioche dough, and baked until golden brown. The end result is an elegant dish that is sure to impress.

Serves 4

1½ to 2 pound wild salmon fillet
3 tablespoons Savory Caramelized Onion Sambal Compote (page 162)
½ recipe Classic Brioche
Egg wash
Kosher salt and freshly ground black pepper, to taste

Preheat oven to 400°F. On a floured work surface, roll out a rectangle of brioche dough that is approximately ¼-inch thick and twice the size of the salmon fillet. Season both sides of the salmon fillet with salt and pepper and place fillet on bottom half of rectangle. Brush top of fillet with the compote and brush the edges of dough lightly with egg wash. Fold the top half of dough over the salmon fillet so that the edges meet and press down to seal all around. Bake for 20 to 25 minutes, until golden brown. Let rest for 5 minutes before slicing and serving.

Serve with: *Cloudy Bay Chardonnay*

JOANNE CHANG'S STICKY BUNS

Serves 6

1 recipe Classic Brioche
1 recipe Goo (below)
2 cups brown sugar
1 teaspoon cinnamon
1 cup pecans, toasted and chopped

Joanne Chang is pastry chef and owner of Boston's incomparable Flour Bakery and droves of people come to this shop for, among other things, her sticky buns. Here she uses her magic touch with my classic brioche dough and covers them with the aptly-named "goo"—a sinfully yummy mixture that includes brown sugar, cream, and butter. These are so good—they are well worth every minute it takes to make them and will leave all other buns far, far behind.

On a floured work surface, roll out the brioche dough into a rectangle that is approximately ¼-inch thick. Combine the brown sugar, cinnamon, and pecans and sprinkle evenly on the brioche. Roll up the brioche jelly roll-style and slice the roll into buns about 1-inch thick. Spread the Goo on the bottom of a roasting pan and place buns evenly spaced in the pan. Cover and allow to rise for 2 to 3 hours in a warm place. Bake in an oven at 350°F until the brioche are golden brown, about 45 minutes. Let cool for 10 minutes and then invert onto a serving platter.

Serve with: *Café au Lait*

GOO
½ pound butter
15 ounces brown sugar
5 ounces honey
½ cup water
½ cup cream

In a saucepan over medium heat, melt together the butter and brown sugar. Remove from heat, let cool, and whisk in the honey, cream, and water. Set aside.

MASTER RECIPE

*This easy custard base gets
its great flavor from fresh ginger
and vanilla beans. While not scientifically
proven, I believe that custard is the most
versatile and popular dessert: ice cream,
crème brûlée, flan, crème caramel, bread
pudding . . . they all use custard in some
form. Here are four different but
equally tasty desserts that
feature this master.*

GINGER VANILLA CUSTARD BASE

Makes 5 cups

> 3½ cups heavy cream
> 1 cup milk
> ¼ cup fresh ginger, peeled and grated
> 2 vanilla beans, split
> 8 egg yolks
> 1 egg
> ⅔ cup sugar

Combine cream, milk, ginger, and vanilla bean in a saucepan over medium heat, and heat until just under scalding—approximately 170°F. While the cream mixture is heating, in a separate bowl whisk together the yolks, whole eggs, and sugar. When the cream mixture has reached the appropriate temperature, temper the yolk mixture by adding a small amount of the hot cream and whisking to warm eggs. Add the heated egg mixture back into the milk and cream mixture and stir to combine.

Pour custard base into a metal container and place in an ice bath, stirring occasionally, then place in the refrigerator. It is best to let the base sit overnight to develop a more intense flavor from vanilla and ginger. Strain the next day or when cold. Store in a container, covered, for 3 to 5 days (depending on the freshness of milk and cream).

RECOMMENDED BEVERAGES

Duck Walk Vineyards, Blueberry Port

Where: Maine
Style: This port is made with hand-picked blueberries from Maine that are small, concentrated, and bursting with flavor, producing a port wine that has intense fruit flavors and is perfect with desserts, especially ones featuring fruit like the Stone fruit Clafoutis.

Jabolet Muscat Beaumes de Venise

Where : Rhone Valley, France
Grape: Muscat
Style: This wine has a pale golden hue and intense fruity and floral aromas. It is full-bodied with lingering fruity aromas and a lemon-tinged finish. It is wonderful with creamy desserts like crème brûlée.

Many people order crème brûlée when dining out. It's special, sweet—but not too sweet—and has that wonderful crackly sugar coating that gives way to a silky custard. This version features the unique addition of ginger for a change from the usual and is easy to make at home. The key is careful baking in a hot water bath. If you really like this dessert, invest in a small propane torch, available at most kitchen supply stores. Brûlée-ing these custards will be much easier and will turn out perfectly every time.

GINGER VANILLA CRÈME BRÛLÉE

Makes twelve 4-ounce or eight 6-ounce ramekins

1 recipe Ginger Vanilla Custard Base
Sugar in the Raw

Preheat oven to 300°F (275°F for convection ovens). Portion custard base into 12 4-ounce ramekins or 8 6-ounce ramekins. Place ramekins in a baking dish and fill with hot water, halfway up the sides of the ramekins. Bake in the water bath for 50 minutes, or until set. Carefully remove from oven and chill completely before serving.

Sprinkle a thin and even layer of sugar over top of custard and brûlée either using a propane torch or under the broiler. Let sit for a minute so the sugar cools and hardens before serving.

Serve with: *Jabolet Muscat Beaumes de Venise*

Bread pudding was most likely conceived as a practical use for stale, day-old bread but we've upped the ante with this version that features brioche-based Five-Spice Coffee Cake soaked in the Ginger Vanilla Custard Base. This bread pudding is, in a word, decadent.

COFFEE CAKE BREAD PUDDING

Serves 6 to 8

1 recipe Ginger Vanilla Custard Base
1 loaf Sweet Five Spiced Coffee Cake (page 164)

Take leftover Sweet Five Spiced Brioche Coffee Cake and cut into ½- or 1-inch cubes. Toast lightly to dry out completely. Portion dried cubes into ramekins or loaf pans two-thirds of the way up. Pour custard base over coffee cake cubes and let sit for several hours in the refrigerator or overnight. Heat oven to 300°F, remove ramekins or loaf pans from the refrigerator and add more custard base to moisten if dry on top. Bake for 30 to 40 minutes or until an inserted knife comes out clean. Served chilled or warm.

Serve with: *Duck Walk Vineyards, Blueberry Port* or *Jabolet Muscat Beaumes de Venise*

Clafoutis is a classic French dessert from Limousin that traditionally is made with cherries but it's delicious with all kinds of fruits (except strawberries which are much too watery!). More custard than cake, this is one of the yummiest ways to eat summer fruits.

STONE FRUIT CLAFOUTIS

Makes six 6-ounce ramekins

1 each, plum, peach, apricot, cut into wedges
18 fresh cherries, pitted and cut in half
8 tablespoons all-purpose flour
¼ teaspoon baking powder
4 tablespoons sugar
¼ teaspoon cinnamon
¼ teaspoon nutmeg
Pinch salt
2½ cups Ginger Vanilla Custard Base

Preheat oven to 350°F and arrange fruit in buttered or greased baking dishes. Combine the dry ingredients in a medium bowl, then very slowly whisk custard base into dry ingredients, two tablespoons at a time, until combined. Pour batter over fruit and bake for 50 minutes or until set. Serve warm with fresh cream or ice cream.

Serve with: *Duck Walk Vineyards Blueberry Port*

JOANNE CHANG'S PROFITEROLES WITH GINGER-VANILLA CREAM

½ pound butter
2 tablespoons sugar
½ teaspoon salt
2 cups water
2 cups all-purpose flour
8 eggs
1 recipe Ganache (see below)
1 recipe Pastry Cream (see next page)

Here Joanne Chang, pastry chef and owner of Flour Bakery, uses the Ginger Vanilla Custard Base to fill profiteroles—what we often refer to as cream puffs—and tops them with a rich chocolate ganache.

Place the butter, sugar, salt and water in a medium saucepan over medium heat. When the liquid comes to a boil, remove from heat and stir in flour with a wooden spoon. Place mixture back on stove and stir vigorously for at least 2 minutes until the mixture forms a film on the bottom of the saucepan. Take mixture off of stove and place in a mixing bowl. Beat with a paddle or by hand for a few seconds to let some steam escape. Slowly beat in eggs, one at a time. Stop adding eggs when the mixture is shiny and holds a soft peak. Pipe onto baking sheets and bake at 400°F for about 10 minutes. Reduce heat to 325°F and continue baking for another 20 to 25 minutes until brown. Let cool on racks and then fill with Pastry Cream and top with Ganache.

Serve with: *Jabolet Muscat Beaumes de Venise*

GANACHE

¼ pound chocolate, roughly chopped
½ cup cream

Place the chocolate in a medium bowl. Heat cream on the stove until just under a boil. Pour the cream over chocolate and stir until smooth. Reserve in a warm place.

PASTRY CREAM

1 recipe Ginger Vanilla Custard Base
⅔ cup sugar
⅔ cup cake flour

Combine the sugar and cake flour and slowly whisk into the Ginger Vanilla Custard Base. Place in a medium saucepan over medium-high heat and whisk continuously until it comes to a boil and continue to whisk vigorously for 30 seconds. Immediately remove from heat and strain through a fine mesh strainer into a container and refrigerate.

Caramel sauce is an
impossibly perfect confection but
this variation, caramel scented with
the heavenly floral jasmine tea, proves that
even perfect things can be improved upon.
Adding this to any dessert will send it into
the next stratosphere. Note that traditionally,
caramel is made with the wet brush method,
but I've borrowed a technique from my pastry chef Marina Brancely, covering the
pot and allowing the condensation
to do its thing.

JASMINE CARAMEL SAUCE

Makes 4 cups

3 cups sugar
¾ cup Jasmine tea, freshly brewed*
½ vanilla bean, scraped into tea
1½ sticks sweet butter, cubed

Place sugar in a heavy-bottomed saucepan and add enough water to make a wet sand mixture. Cover with top and heat sugar mixture over medium-high heat until it starts to color. Remove top and allow to continue cooking until it turns a deep amber but pay attention once sugar starts to turn, as the process happens quite fast! Once sugar has caramelized as desired, turn off the heat and slowly add the tea, pouring it gently down the side of the pot. Whisk in the butter, returning to heat and allowing mixture to dissolve and become smooth again.

*Note: Brew 4 tea bags in 8 ounces of water, strain and add scraped vanilla bean. If you can, use whole leaf tea—it produces a stronger, more fragrant tea needed to flavor this caramel sauce.

RECOMMENDED BEVERAGES

Pedro Ximenez Sherry

Where: Alvear, Spain
Grape: Sherry is made from Pedro Ximenez Raisins
Style: This is a syrupy pure sherry with a delicate fluency and it is perfect with desserts—a rich elixir for any moment!

Ambazillac Cuvee Mademoiselle

Where : Bordeaux, France
Grape: 80% sauvignon blanc, 20% semillon
Style: This is a well-balanced dessert wine with a bright color, floral nose, noticeable acidity, and not-too-sweet finish that is particularly good with creamy desserts such as ice cream and crème brûlée.

TOASTED ALMOND TEA CAKE

Makes 16 4-ounce mini loaves

4 cups all-purpose flour
1 cup almond flour, toasted
3 cups sugar
2 teaspoons baking powder
2 teaspoons salt
6 eggs, large
1½ cups canola oil
1 tablespoon vanilla extract
1 cup Jasmine Caramel Sauce
1 recipe Streusel (recipe follows)
2 cups sliced almonds

STREUSEL

6 ounces oats, old-fashioned
9 ounces butter, cold, cubed
6 ounces bread flour
6 ounces brown sugar, dark
6 ounces sugar

Toast almond flour, cool. Combine other dry ingredients, set aside. Make the Streusel filling by combining the dry ingredients with a paddle attachment in a stand mixer, then cutting in cold butter. Mix until crumbly, being careful not to over mix! Set aside.

Finish making the tea cake by combining the eggs, oil, and vanilla extract with a whip attachment on a KitchenAid mixer. Fold the egg mixture and flour mixture together. Pour batter into greased pans, swirl with the Jasmine Caramel Sauce and top with Streusel. Bake at 325°F until just set, approximately 30 to 40 minutes. Remove from oven and cool.

Serve with: *Pedro Ximenez Sherry* or a cup of steaming hot *Jasmine Tea*

This tea cake has a delicate texture and wonderful flavor thanks to toasted almond flour. Before baking, Jasmine Caramel Sauce is swirled into the batter and then it's topped with a buttery sweet streusel. One warning: you won't be able to have just one slice!

Ice cream sundaes are an amazing food: they combine hot and cold, crunchy and smooth. Bananas are a fruit made for caramel and combined and poured over vanilla ice cream creates one of the most incredible spoonfuls of yumminess in this world. Just a sprinkle of almonds are needed to complete this treat.

JASMINE BANANA CARAMEL SAUCE FOR ICE CREAM SUNDAES

Makes 1 quart

1 recipe Jasmine Caramel Sauce, reduced by 50 percent
3 fresh bananas, sliced
Vanilla ice cream
Toasted almond slices

Place sliced bananas in a medium bowl and pour warm caramel sauce over them. Keep warm until ready to use and serve with vanilla ice cream, garnished with toasted almonds. The caramel sauce can be prepared a week in advance, however the bananas should be added the same day as serving.

Note: For a truly amazing sundae, top slices of the Toasted Almond Tea Cake with ice cream, spoon Jasmine Banana Caramel Sauce over, and garnish with toasted almonds and Toasted Sesame Nougat Bark. Wow!

Serve with: *Ambazillac Cuvée Mademoiselle*

In addition to sauces, caramel is the basis for many soft and hard candies. This one features toasted sesame seeds—a common ingredient in many Chinese sweets. It's then dipped into dark chocolate or served ungarnished. This is perfect when you are looking for a "little something" to have at the close of a meal or with a cup of tea.

TOASTED SESAME NOUGAT BARK

Recipe Yields: Two 13- x 9-inch pans

1 recipe Jasmine Caramel Sauce
1 cup toasted sesame seeds
Dark chocolate (optional)

Reduce caramel sauce by 50 percent over medium-low heat, heating to almost the hard-crack stage. Stir in sesame seeds and pour out onto a sheet pan lined with greased parchment paper. Let cool.

Break into random pieces for bite size candies and dip into melted chocolate, or chop and use for garnish on ice cream sundaes.

Serve with: *Pedro Ximenez Sherry*

Ming and chef Gale Gand sample their work.

GALE GAND'S PEAR TARTE TATIN

Serves 6 to 8

1 sheet puff pastry
1 recipe Jasmine Caramel Sauce, reduced by 50 percent
1 cinnamon stick
2 tablespoons vanilla brandy
2 tablespoons orange juice
4 to 5 ripe pears, peeled, halved and seed packet removed with a melon baller
Whipped cream or ice cream for serving

Tarte Tatin is a classic French dessert served at many bistros and cafes in France. Gale Gand, a world-class pastry chef, TV host, and cookbook author uses pears instead of apples and scents the Jasmine Caramel with orange, vanilla brandy, and cinnamon. This golden syrupy tart is gorgeous to look at and even better to eat—especially when served slightly warm with a scoop of vanilla bean ice cream—yum . . .

Preheat oven to 425°F.

Thaw the sheet of puff pastry and cut a round disk out using a 9-inch cake pan as your guide but cut it 1-inch bigger all around. In the same 9-inch cake pan, warm the caramel over medium heat until it starts to bubble. Add the cinnamon stick and stir to combine. Stir in the brandy and orange juice to deglaze the pan and continue cooking until it becomes a smooth caramel. Remove the cake pan from the heat and then place the pear halves in the pan in a spoke pattern.

Return the pan to the stove and cook on low for 20 minutes to tenderize the pears somewhat. Top the pears with the round of puff pastry, draping it over the edge of the pan (don't worry, it will shrink during baking). Bake 20 to 25 minutes at 425°F, or until the pastry is golden brown. Let cool in the pan to set the caramel. The pectin the fruit has given off will help set the juices. Turn upside down onto a plate and remove the pan to serve. You may need to warm the bottom of the pan slightly over a hot burner to allow the tart to release from the pan. Serve warm or at room temperature, in slices, with a dollop of whipped cream or scoop of ice cream.

Serve with: *Ambazillac Cuvée Mademoiselle* or cup of *Dark Roasted Coffee*

*Salsas are not only savory—
some can be sweet such as this
lychee-cranberry version which combines
two fruits from opposite sides of the world:
the New England cranberry and the Far
East lychee. This versatile salsa may also
be transformed into a warm compote or
puréed and frozen into a myriad
of cold confections.*

LYCHEE-CRANBERRY SALSA

Makes 1 quart

| 2 cans lychees, strained
| 1 bag cranberries
| ½ cup sugar
| Zest of 1 orange, finely chopped
| Juice of 1 orange
| 2 teaspoons vanilla extract

Combine all ingredients in a food processor and blend until medium-coarse in texture.

Tip: In addition to using this master in some delicious desserts, the Lychee-Cranberry Salsa is great as an accompaniment to pork or poultry dishes.

RECOMMENDED BEVERAGES

De Trafford "Straw Wine"

Where: Stellenbosch, South Africa
Grape: Chenin Blanc
Style: This wine gets its unique name from the process of laying out the grapes on straw mats to dry, thereby concentrating the sugar and fruit, creating intense flavors of apricot and honey while maintaining an acidic balance. This is not overly sweet like many botrytised wines and it manages to be fruity without being rich.

Joao Pires Muscat

Where: Sebutal, Portugal
Grape: Muscat
Style: This semi-dry Muscat comes from the hotter area of Portugal where the grapes get very ripe. This produces slightly floral, musky notes. This is a great to serve as an aperitif or on a hot summer day—especially with fruits and ices.

One of my favorite desserts is ice cream and cold vanilla ice cream served with a warm fruit compote is a great contrast of temperatures. This Lychee-Cranberry Salsa gets bumped up a notch with the addition of raspberries which add more berry flavor and wonderful texture to this compote.

VANILLA ICE CREAM WITH WARM LYCHEE-CRANBERRY-RASPBERRY COMPOTE

Serves 4 to 6

1 recipe Lychee-Cranberry Salsa
¼ cup cranberry juice
2 pints fresh raspberries
Vanilla ice cream

Cook the salsa over low heat with cranberry juice until soft. Remove from heat and add the raspberries. Serve warm with ice cream and fresh cream.

Serve with: *De Trafford Straw Wine*

Growing up, my mom always made homemade popsicles in those Tupperware molds with orange and cranberry juices, convinced it was healthier. Using this Salsa plus cran-raspberry juice yields a more sophisticated flavor and some more grown up frozen desserts including a smooth granita with champagne and colorful ice cubes for cocktails and punches.

LYCHEE-CRANBERRY-RASPBERRY GRANITA, POPSICLES, AND ICE CUBES

Makes 3 quarts

1 recipe Lychee-Cranberry Salsa
32 ounces cran-raspberry juice
Veuve Clicquot Champagne (for Granita)

Put Lychee-Cranberry Salsa in a food processor and blend until smooth. Strain into a bowl and add cran-raspberry juice.

For Granita: add 1 cup of champagne for every quart of Lychee-Cranberry-Raspberry mixture and freeze in a shallow baking dish. Once frozen, scrape surface with a large spoon and place scoops of the shavings in martini glasses. Pour ¼ cup of champagne over granita and serve.

For Popsicles: Freeze in appropriate molds or make your own with wooden craft sticks purchased from your local craft store, and paper cups.

For Ice Cubes: freeze in any size and shape desired and use in your favorite cocktail or summer coolers. Particularly delicious in a pitcher of lemonade!

Serve with: *Joao Pires Muscat*

Strawberry shortcake is a classic American dessert especially popular during the summer months. Here is an equally delicious version with lychees and cranberries. If you don't have time to make the shortcake biscuits, you may purchase them at a bakery.

LYCHEE-CRANBERRY SHORTCAKE

Serves 4

4 sweet biscuits (recipe follows)
2 cups Lychee-Cranberry Salsa
2 cups sweetened whipped cream

Split biscuits in half horizontally and place a generous spoonful of Salsa on bottom half. Place biscuit half on top and cover with more Salsa and whipped cream. Garnish with a mint sprig if desired.

SWEET BISCUITS — Makes twenty-four 2½- to 3-inch biscuits

1 stick plus 4 tablespoons butter, very cold
2½ cups bread flour
2½ cups cake flour
2 teaspoons salt
1 tablespoon baking powder
⅔ cup sugar

Zest of 1 lemon, grated
2 eggs
2 cups heavy cream
2 teaspoons vanilla extract
Heavy cream and Sugar in the Raw

Preheat oven to 350°F. Cube butter into walnut size pieces, set aside in refrigerator. Combine dry ingredients and lemon zest in a stand mixer. Mix butter into dry ingredients with a paddle attachment until butter is broken down in size a bit, but is not fully mixed in. Combine eggs, cream and vanilla extract in a separate bowl and whisk together. Add egg mixture slowly to the flour mixture until well incorporated, but not over mixed. Place dough on a lightly floured surface, form a loose ball and cover in plastic. Allow dough to rest in the refrigerator for 30 minutes. Remove from refrigerator and place on a floured work surface. Roll dough to ½-inch thickness, give it one "book-fold", roll back out to ½-inch and cut into desired size for shortcakes. Put shortcakes on a parchment lined or greased baking sheet, brush with heavy cream and sprinkle with "Sugar in the Raw". Bake for approximately 20 to 30 minutes, or until golden brown. Remove from oven and cool.

Note: Dough freezes well.

Serve with: *De Trafford Straw Wine*

GALE GAND'S FROZEN PASSION FRUIT PARFAIT

Serves 6 to 8

Gale Gand, pastry guru, made this elegant passion fruit terrine on the program, which is a great way to enjoy a homemade ice cream dessert without having to use an ice cream maker. The tropical sweet-tart flavor of passion fruit is awesome paired with the Lychee-Cranberry Salsa. You may find Gale at her restaurant Tru in Chicago.

4 egg yolks
½ cup sugar
2 tablespoons honey
6 tablespoons milk
6 tablespoons passion fruit purée (Goya brand is available in the Latino frozen section)
½ vanilla bean
1¾ cups heavy cream, whipped
1 recipe Lychee-Cranberry Salsa

Grease a terrine mold with butter and then line with parchment paper. In a stainless steel mixing bowl whisk together the yolks, sugar, honey, milk, passion fruit purée, and vanilla bean and cook over simmering water until frothy and light like a sabayon. Let cool slightly and then fold in the whipped cream. Pour into the parchment lined mold, wrap in plastic wrap and freeze. Turn out the next day and peel off the paper. On a dessert plate serve a slice, cut in half diagonally topped with a spoonful of the Salsa.

Serve with: *Joao Pires Muscat*

Thank you to our Funders
for making SIMPLY MING possible.

All-Clad Metalcrafters, Inc.

Clicquot, Inc.

Contessa Food Products

Ocean Spray Cranberries, Inc.

Additional thanks to:

Brioni at Louis Boston

Clarke

Front of the House

Grace Lee Design

Hiroshima

Lower Falls Wine Company

Melissa's World Variety Produce

Sub-Zero & Wolf

Acorn Kitchens, Ltd. ◆ Armstrong Flooring ◆ Asko, Inc. ◆ Captain Marden's Seafoods ◆ Chefwear ◆
Courtyard Boston Milford ◆ Cuisipro ◆ Dav El Chauffeured Transportation Network ◆ East Meets West Catering ◆
Emile Henry ◆ The New Hotel Commonwealth ◆ John Boos & Co. ◆ KitchenAid Home Appliances ◆
KWC Sinks & Faucets ◆ Kyocera Advanced Ceramics ◆ Maui Floral ◆ Mystic Mountain Orchids ◆
New England Stone, Inc. ◆ Niman Ranch ◆ Super 88 Markets ◆ T.F. Kinnealey & Co., Inc. ◆
TriMark United East/Libbey Glassware ◆ Whole Foods Market